TO DIE IN CHICAGO

Nadja Tesich

iUniverse, Inc.
New York   Bloomington

To Die in Chicago

iUniverse books may be ordered through booksellers or by contacting:
iUniverse
1663 Liberty Drive
Bloomington, IN 47403
www.iuniverse.com
1-800-Authors (1-800-288-4677)

A special thanks to the Yaddo Colony and MacDowell Colony
where Nadja Tesich worked on this book.

ISBN: 978-1-4502-3389-7 (pbk)
ISBN: 978-1-4502-3390-3 (ebk)

Printed in the United States of America
iUniverse rev. date: 8/11/10

*To all my families, to my mother, my son Stefan
and his children, and all of my friends*

In special memory of my brother Steve Tesich

Chapter One

The first thing you notice about East Chicago is the acrid smell of sulphur, like boiled eggs. Black dust covers everything; all the trees are gray. From the refineries nearby, red flames shoot up, an amazing sight at night. That's what I saw later, each time I came, but not right away, not that time. Only the smell was there. That first day I am too stunned to pay attention, we've been on the ship for five days and nobody understands anything we say, a week on Ellis Island and all those X-rays, finally twenty-four hours on the train to get to this place, our final destination. In Hollywood films immigrants usually arrive in New York harbor wearing folk costumes, bundles in their hands, they cry from happiness and kiss the land. In real life, at least in our case, it didn't happen like that, and there was no background music suggesting that the film will end soon and our wonderful new life will begin.

When the train stopped and we got out, Mother dragging one suitcase, me the other, this short frail man (shorter than my memory, my imagination of him) was waiting for us but he didn't look like anyone I knew. He wore a beige raincoat which appeared too big for him, an old double-breasted suit of a grayish shade, his hair was brown, his eyes blue — this was my father I had not seen for years. Before I could go through the motions I had imagined many times at home, how it was all supposed to be and music stolen from movies would play as we wept, unable to stop, Mother pushed me toward him and I was in his arms and maybe he had tears in his eyes when he said, "You are the only one who still looks the same. Nothing about your face has changed." I didn't know if this was good or bad.

So, nothing lived up to our imagination from the beginning; the meeting was ordinary, nobody wept, he looked crumpled or maybe he was disappointed too. I didn't think about all this right away, how could I, tired and stunned, know that his words to me were an insult to her, my Mother, how could I know those things at fifteen, I who had never kissed anyone yet, had never lived around men. Later, much later, when it was too late to know him, I would dream about that figure at the train station and he appeared over and over again to bother me in the dreams that wouldn't stop. In them he was never dead but only pretending; he was hiding, running away from her. The dreams lasted an eternity, my entire youth, my thirties too, and I searched for him in real life but never found him in other men. In these dreams about him, he took me to the most exotic places, to Northern Africa or what looked like it, the sea in the background, and there he wore a white hat in a long shot far away; in Paris he disappeared around Saint Michel waving his hand, see you later. The last time he showed up, the only time he ever came near enough so I could see his face, we were in some ugly apartment with a formica table in the middle, and I ran up to him and said, "Dad, guess what, I've become a writer—funny isn't it?" I expected him to react, something big to happen, but he only looked at me, smiled his same old smile, kind of sad, then shook my hand across the table. And that was that. He had never done anything similar in real life, so I decided in the dream he was pleased. He liked books too. He never showed up again, maybe I've stopped calling him, chasing him all over the globe.

The same year my dreams ended, the film modeled on our lives was shot in Chicago, and I saw his grave for the first time. We were in

2

a cemetery full of dead Serbs and all of us had turned into Hollywood characters — he, fair and small-boned, was played by a swarthy guy with huge shoulders and a moustache; Mother, dark in real life, was now pale blonde; my brother, played by a young blond actor, had the main part, while portions of my life were given to an American girl who couldn't dance and behaved on screen like a little slut. In a picture above his grave, Dad stared ahead, oblivious to all this, so sweet-looking in his cadet's uniform, so very young. It was the time I didn't know, before the war and marriage, before me. What did he think about that day as he posed for this picture? Not about his grave, that's for sure.

There is no way to know what he thought that day at the train station either, and my own thoughts are gone. Most likely they were not there, the way it is with kids or primitive people. Sensations in the body instead, hot, hungry, tired, where am I? I am a girl in an indigo blue dress, a pretty wool dress of the right length for my age, knees visible, my hair is long, blond, and my eyes are blue as always. That's what he saw that day, most likely, his daughter still the same. He must have been happy about that, and he probably recognized the indigo material of my dress because he had bought it, sent it for me after all.

The landscape from inside the car didn't resemble any American film we had seen, neither a Western with red earth, horses, big skies, nor the other ones with flowers and swimming pools where Liz, Grace, and all those stars lived. All my girlfriends copied their haircuts, they even wrote letters to Hollywood begging for a photo of their favorites, then they spent hours foolishly comparing themselves, wondering if their legs, their waists were as long, as small, as perfect. Not me. Who can say why not, maybe because Hollywood didn't seem real; like science fiction, it didn't have the smell of earth in it, or because I liked my own country or because I preferred books, and they told of another America which was not just blue and white but shades of gray. Still, I was not prepared for what I saw that day. No writer had described it and even if they had, it wouldn't be the same because a book is only a book, you can start another one, or you can go and see a friend and then you can go swimming after lunch. The books have clear beginnings and ends, it's different. Outside, through the windows of that car, it was all gray, white gray like old people, then darker shades of coal toward the factories, and that smell of sulphur. It tickled your throat. It made your eyes itch.

We said nothing to each other but we must have seen the house in the same way — gray wood, paint peeling, tarpaper, the grayest place ever. At home the houses were made to last for a long time, either in brick or stone, except for the mountain huts or those ski chalets in bright colors, yellow, green, red. The man who drove the car mumbled something to my father, then left.

We followed him, through the front door, up the narrow staircase to the second floor apartment he had rented. A dog howled next door, then somebody shouted back. This was our new home.

It was May, hot already. My blue dress was perfect for spring days at home, with all those mountains and the river, even summer nights were fresh. We slept with blankets on, and you had to have a jacket after sunset. It was that kind of climate, neither too hot nor too cold, but what is this misery, and in May? Stojan wiped his forehead, poor thing, all decked out in his first suit, wool too, a jacket with short pants, wool knee socks; he even wore a real shirt and tie.

There were four rooms, one in the back had a large bed, a smaller one to the left with a funny green sofa you opened by pulling on this belt, you took out the pillow and the sheets, spread them, slept, then you took it all off, and stuffed it under. That's how people sleep here, he said. I didn't like it right away. All that pushing, pulling you had to do, every day. Our beds always stayed put, always in the same spot, in the cool room full of embroidered things. In our bedroom the view extended through the window, always open in the summer, across the trees, all the way to the creek, big foamy, whispering in the spring when the snow begins to melt. At home I heard the spring as I slept.

In the living room for which we didn't have a word because we really lived in the kitchen, there was another olive green couch you had to open with a belt. Stojan looked disappointed—that's where he would sleep. You could tell he didn't like it either because he didn't have a room of his own or that he would be separated from us. At home all three of us slept together in two large beds pushed together which were a part of Mother's trousseau she rescued in pieces after the bombing, then a friendly carpenter glued everything all back, so well nobody could ever tell. I could see Stojan was unhappy and for a reason. It wasn't fair that Mother and I had presents waiting for us — something called 'a house coat', slippers to match, while it hadn't occurred to Father to buy similar things for him, or a toy a boy would like. He didn't know much about boys and he himself didn't have slippers or housecoats at twelve and most likely nobody ever gave him a toy. Even though they said I was very smart, I was not smart enough to consider all this at fifteen. Later yes. At that moment I only thought not fair, governed then and now by some system of just and unjust left over from my old school and my grandma who divided everything evenly, like a just God, or how I imagined perfect socialism would be. Everything I do has some of her in it, even this book is for her, it has to be. I thought about her that first day in that apartment, where would she sleep if she had come with us, if she were alive. I called her to help me the way she always did. She had rescued me from Germans, she knew exactly what to say to persuade the killers not to kill me. I never think dead when I think about her, the moment I say grandma she is in the room either in front of me or by my shoulder with that smell of woods about her.

In this new kitchen the air smells of dust, nothing you can attach yourself to. My eyes shut, I try to see her face. When I manage, I am still me. She'll guide me. Help me, I say inside of myself. She would have slept in the kitchen but this one didn't have a bed even though it was huge in comparison with the other, you could dance in this one. A table has a shiny white top and legs of a peculiar shape, fat ungraceful, shiny too. Aluminum he said, formica, easy to clean, just wipe it. True, nothing to it, so much easier than the wood, ugly though, so ugly.

Chairs had the same funny legs with bright red seats, four of them. By the door the black object was the stove; it functioned with oil, he said. The oil is in the basement, you carry it up, you pour it inside, then you light a match. Not now, in the winter. The white kitchen sink with hot and cold water was certainly new for us although we had seen it before in the new apartments on the main street. We, like all the others in our neighborhood, only had a pump in the back yard, cold, clear mountain water, the longer you pump the colder it gets, pump it for a long time for your guest, serve it in a glass on a silver tray with coffee and cherry preserves. That's the first thing you offer, when someone visits, then this or that, always with pauses in between.

"You put the water in the fridge, in a milk bottle or any other," he said, introducing a white object next to the sink. It was fat and it hummed in a strange way. Nobody had a fridge at home, and even though it made everything easy for Mother, it was ugly, made too much noise. We didn't need it before. She bought everything fresh at the market in the morning, and we had fresh eggs from our own chickens, which woke you up at dawn. Sometimes I snuck in before her and drank a new egg through a straw; sometimes we did it together, Stojan and I, but we didn't take all of them—just one each. You can only do that with the freshest eggs, not those in the fridge, and Dad said in America the eggs are made with machines. We are not impressed with this fridge thing, even though you could store up meat, milk, cheese, shop only once a week, save time—but who wants to save time if it was more fun the other way, and you saw everyone at the market, your friends, peasants, horses with carts, gypsies arguing, and pigs that were alive. Sure the gas stove next to the fridge was much easier to use, no doubt about it, rather than chopping wood, starting the fire in the morning, my job, but here you had to worry about the gas, he said, make sure it's properly lit. "It could kill you," he said. "Make sure, don't forget." He showed us how to do it with matches, pouf it went in the oven. It could kill you, I kept thinking that first day. You could die in this kitchen.

Now, the bathtub should have made everyone happy, so big, so white, so nice. Nobody around us had one like this, although we had seen them in the new apartments on the main street. Still, we should be impressed, but we are thinking it's summer, who needs a bath if you can swim in the river, what's a bathtub if you can sit under the falls and, if you wish, drink the flowing water. At that moment we are not thinking about the winter when the river is frozen and Mother had to warm the water on the stove, pour it into the wooden tub where the laundry was done, too. Fortunately for her, we had a full bath only once a week. Then she used that water to wash her underwear and our socks, or to clean the floor. Here we could wash any time we wanted to, we could sit in the tub forever, or let the water run up to the brim. And the new toilet was so much easier than walking to our john, in the garden, in the snow at night. Somewhere there amongst the trees the ghosts were hidden, the souls of dead girls whispered through the planks, wind carried their voices urging you to jump. Jump jump, come with me, they said on the edge of the ravine, come closer, their voices said. There, in the sunlight, it was all different. Below, through the bushes by the creek, peasant women stopped to pee just lifting their skirts up, with no worries about toilets or staying clean.

Here in Chicago we could wash as much as we wanted, and Mother would have a machine, he said, and then the machine would do it all. Everything was easier, no doubt about it — water, tub, gas, fridge, sitting down on a white toilet seat, yet it didn't make anyone happier or overjoyed for some reason, not even a bit. Somehow we were not astonished by these things the way we were expected to be, they failed to produce that funny ski- and-jump feeling in your chest when, running into the house Stojan said, "Guess what's at the movies tonight!" or when we woke up and the sky was without a single cloud and that meant swimming the whole day at the river or swimming first, then movies later, why not. That feeling of joy, of being alive, of summer light, that something I don't have the right word for. In this new place we are too tired, is that it? We don't know what it is; we don't

7

dare think what now. Maybe it was the grayness of it, every house alike and that smell of rotten eggs and that sharp whistle of the factory twice a day. Maybe a pretty landscape of trees, ocean, and big blue sky would have startled us, seduced us, and then we would have liked the fridge and the stove too. No, not really. What good are all those things if you can't yell through the window, come play with us, come have some warm bread. She didn't bake just for us. The bread with the brown crust, hard on the outside, soft inside, was better than butter, steak, better than anything. It had the smell we knew.

We didn't think happy or unhappy, that word was not used that much. It was an animal feeling in the stomach of something awful, bigger than the biggest disappointment. Did we leave everything for this? Is this it? Most likely that's what we thought, if any thought occurred to us. Our faces must have looked the same, Mother's had gloom written all over it, even Stojan so cheerful in general had a new expression that resembled grief. This new feeling around us was more dreadful than the memory of war, or the poverty after, worse than Grandma's death, worse than anything because you didn't know what to call it. Disappointment is too slender. Before, we were together with others; neighbors came to celebrate all of it, my good grades, death, weddings, and births. This, where we sat, was an unknown misery nobody could imagine or name, nothing had prepared us for it in that small town by the river. That's why we didn't know what to do, how to fight it, make it better. It wasn't our fault really.

It was her decision. I had nothing to do with it, nobody had asked me. In fact I didn't want to go, and why should I when everything was so perfect — the best student, the best pioneer too, just when I was falling in love with a boy who was dark, handsome, and looked like a gypsy. And the worst of it, he hadn't even kissed me yet, not even once. If at least I had done that part. That failed kiss will haunt me for years, always, and no matter how much I kissed it would never be the kiss I wanted, the one that should have happened, didn't, yet was more real than all the other ones.

8

She didn't think about all this when she decided to have us together after so many years. What would my kiss mean when her worries were bigger, why would a head of state think about entertainment if he has to think about the price of wheat. Stojan needs a father, she kept saying, or he'll go wild. How can I manage alone? She cried. If she had managed all alone before, why couldn't she continue? I kept thinking, and we are all grown up. Who knows what her reasons were, maybe she didn't know for sure. She gave all sorts of reasons later on, she often said she had wanted to come to America since she was a child; it was a happy land her father had loved, the country full of gold and no wars, but I couldn't tell if this was the main reason or her fear that Stojan would turn into a bum.

Her father didn't end well. He left healthy for California where he dug for gold, then became sick and came home to die.

Stojan, in whose name the departure was planned, was the only one not sad to leave; he was too young to have any regrets about a lost love, like me — already at fifteen that word 'lost' permanently in the back of my head — nor did he cry like Mama about her sister, her friends and Grandma's grave on the hillside. At home, graves have to be watched over; dead people expect constant visits and care. But to be fair, how do I know what Stojan thought, poor thing so hot in his suit, too stunned to show anything. Still, he must have had all sorts of dreams of his own about this man he had never known, a strong, wonderful father who would guide, protect, offer gifts and many hugs; in his games Stojan often traveled to America; he also loved to show off with a rubber ball he had received once. That red ball, neither too big nor too small, was the first rubber ball for us, how happy he was with it, how popular on the street. It did create a few problems with the kids who only had rag balls, and the pretty red one was found cut in half one morning. My own dreams of America were not any personal wishes but largely images stolen from the screen, and because I expected nothing from America, nothing at all, I can still bring back those imaginary pictures of it, snapshots in my mind —just close your eyes and you'll see — this other America that's sort of pink, like lipsticks and nail polish, and there are turquoise swimming pools. In the background the soft music plays; closer still, young girls in foamy white dresses whirl and kiss. The sound of the ocean is there too, and water glistens even when it's dark. Which film is this? Was Elizabeth Taylor in it?

That first day, the apartment smelled of old dust accumulated in those sofas and the carpet, gray with red flowers. On the radio, however, on the immigrant station, we heard a song Father had dedicated to us, to tell others we had come. He did think about this detail, being a sentimental kind. The man on the radio sang a Bosnian song about happy love, a rare song for Bosnia where all loves are unhappy.

Somebody must have cooked for us that first day but I can't recollect the person or the food. In the afternoon, men appeared in twos or threes to look at us. They had heard the song on the radio.

They didn't look like people we knew, hefty, red-faced, their suits tight around the shoulders. They looked uncomfortable in them. Most were simple peasants who had through some trick of destiny landed here in the mills, either because they were prisoners in Germany or had retreated with the royal army as the new, Communist era began. At home, peasants were scrawny, silent, light on their feet, not at all like these guys who after a drink or two wept, pinched cheeks, drank some more, and gave dollars to Stojan and me. They had things on their minds, their kids, their cows, their old fields. We were the first to arrive; they couldn't keep their hands off us. Everything about us was beautiful, my skin so white, my sandals they touched and admired the leather. All our clothes were home made, by someone we knew, and this included my pleated skirt and Mother's dress with polka dots, Stojan's shirts, everything, even our sandals.

I had never seen so many men together in one room and crying for no reason. Their cows had sweet names, my Blackie, my Golden, they said, their fields smelled of clover, willows, here even violets have no smell, they moaned. Later, I would notice that too but couldn't decide why they didn't smell at all even though they looked the same. That day we were better than violets to them, that's why they sniffed at us so much, we must have had a smell they remembered.

Some of these men had wives and children at home while others were too young to get married when the war started and they couldn't marry an American woman because she'll divorce you and get your money they said. It happened to this man they knew. So, through no fault of their own, they had skipped the most important part in their lives, the time to marry, have children, and become real men. They didn't know who they were any more, and how could you if flowers have no smell and women are without passion. Maybe dad said that. Without passion, I thought, not understanding much. And the day ended somehow. That sofa bed was hard, uncomfortable with a dividing line in the middle. It never became a real bed. I only slept in it, that's all.

I don't trust books or people who tell you rationally, in great detail, with perfect order, how they felt, who they were when young. Kids don't think that way and memory is not intellectual. You add that later on to fabricate an acceptable version, the preferred story of your life for you and the others but it has nothing to do with original moments, gone, forgotten along with you. When you are young, the world is hazy, without clear shape or words, you don't control it. Only senses are real; for me the sound and smell where portions of my past are hidden can be revived. Maybe. If I get lucky. Thanks to the smell of a certain perfume, or lipstick no longer found in the stores, I remembered that first summer, the parts seemingly dead. That's why I chased after a tall brunette on a subway, but she disappeared, leaving me with the scent of cheap perfume from one of those five-and-ten stores: I should have kept perfume bottles, powders, lipsticks as a guide. Photos reveal nothing, no matter how interesting. I stare and stare and still a zero. Who is that, I say about my own picture. Just a young girl, it could be anyone. Perfume bottles should be kept. If you go back, nothing can be found, not even the smell. Buildings get replaced — instead of that ten-cent store in East Chicago, you now see a parking lot. That time no longer exists, even my school is gone, not that I regret it, not even a tiny bit. Didn't I imagine it burnt to the ground, blown up? And my old home and country no longer exist either; Yugoslavia fell apart in '91. I must be writing this to preserve something, for whom I wonder. I wouldn't be doing it if I saw a book like this in print.

I wonder if she displeased him right away, if it was mutual or if it happened because of the heat as the temperature reached one hundred degrees and we felt like dying, unable to sleep. If only it had been cooler, if only this or that, I thought later, silly games, pointless, you'll never know. My view is limited by everything I don't know. Just like Yugoslavia these days. I could swear we loved each other or maybe we did when I was a kid and now they scream no, not true.

What were they like alone together, for example, but even if I knew that part, it still wouldn't amount to much, I'd have to be inside their heads, a hard thing to do if it's so hard to recapture the small portion — what was in mine. There is no memory of food that day, just heat, the end of May, three of us dressed in wool clothes which would be thrown away very soon. But that first day this has not happened yet, we are dressed in our homemade clothes, as the immigrant station plays that song, "Here comes my love and joy," and nobody is arguing yet.

People came and went late into the night. When did it all start? Maybe right away, as soon as the last visitor left, maybe it was all there that first day already, just waiting to explode. After all, she wasn't pleased that all those men singled me out, raved about my skin, my eyes, and said nothing about her. They should have, I would have liked it better. She expected it, most likely, not so much the part about skin and eyes but more important stuff; she wanted Father to say in front of others how courageous she had been, to raise us so well and with no help from anyone. Just her own hands. Kids don't grow like weeds, oh no, she said, it takes nights and days of hard work, a woman alone with worries about grandma and Janja too, in a country left ravaged by the war and all that without a single blemish on her reputation, not like some sluts.

The men did say what wonderful kids we were but none asked her about her suffering, what others at home knew. Her old stories had to be told, become known to give her a history, who she had been up to now. How else could they know her, judge her without her heroic parts? She couldn't volunteer all this, she had to be properly introduced, but it wasn't done, and the men just went on and on about my hair. The recognition she deserved, she didn't get. It wasn't fair. And it was so easy to do, easier than my missed kiss. He should have praised her for everything: her faithfulness, her youth spent on us. Did he ever appreciate this, I wonder, or did he only see a woman with deep wrinkles on her forehead, around her eyes, even though she was still young?

Handsome really, but not the young girl he had left. That, she couldn't be. Maybe that was the reason why I saw a new expression on her face, and her words seemed strange to me at fifteen when she said to those guys, "Sure she is pretty but I was much prettier than her. I was so strong," she said using a peasant expression which implied beauty with strength, "so pretty that if you slapped one of my cheeks, the other one would have burst." It meant she used to have very round cheeks, and in addition she was angry, now, with me. It's not my fault, I did nothing, I kept thinking.

Chapter Two

I don't think about Ellis Island very much or, if I did, it was in passing because we only stayed there for ten days or maybe it was for a week. There is a museum there now about immigration, and we must have been among the last to go through this place which received, examined, and accepted or rejected all those people from various ships. It's hard to imagine what was it like for them, like cattle, days and days across the ocean, women nursing, old people dying, the dead thrown overboard. Our case was very different. We didn't suffer on the Queen Elizabeth, a ship with twelve floors; dance bands every night, more food than you could ever eat. Father had arranged all this, and we were never supposed to stop at Ellis Island at all.

If I still think about that place, it's only because nobody believed me later and that includes various professors of history from CUNY. I must have imagined it, they said, they have never heard such a thing. In the museum now I can still recognize the immense hall and the stairs that led to the rooms above where we slept. My vertigo, my fear at the museum is the guide to memory, a blur of days merged together, we were confused, didn't expect this to happen, why did they single us on arrival, the only ones? Who are these men in uniform? Why are they silent? A car with us and these cops sped across New York, gray looking through the glass. An empty ferry boat, just us, took us to the Island which looked like a prison of sorts. We had known nothing about it before. If I have interrupted the story of East Chicago with this short chapter, it's because it was a prelude to things later on, an America of the fifties we knew nothing about. Without that climate, my life would have been different, even if every other detail had remained the same. In this respect, this is not just my story or it's mine with forces in the background playing a big part. We understood nothing. Were we kidnapped? At some point this bold guy tried to explain that it had to do with disease and how they wanted to make sure we were free of it. It made no sense, what disease. An embassy doctor saw us in Belgrade, their dentist examined our teeth, we were told months ahead that all the cavities had to be filled. We had none, Stojan and I. Now, this man is trying to tell us through an interpreter who only knows a few words that they want to make sure we are not cheating. Not about teeth but lungs. That doctor did a bad job apparently, because on the X-ray a part of Mother's left lung was missing and they worried she might have TB, and if she had TB they didn't want to pay for it, nor did they want other Americans infected. So they had to do it all over, but not just hers. We, Stojan and I, were forced to have X-rays again even though we didn't have any parts of our lungs missing. Even if I accept all this, fine, but why should all this take ten days or a week?

The immense hall of the museum was jam-packed then with all sorts of people who sat or slept in their chairs. Kids shouted in different languages, babies nursed; we understood no one. In the morning we were permitted to go outside but there was nowhere to go. A few steps in this direction or that; there were limits to how far we could go. In front of our building, in a large field, men played soccer and said things to us. They were separated from us by a wall of barbed wire; their case had to be worse than ours, except we didn't know what they had done. After they had played for an hour, guards took them away. We didn't have a guard. Days must have passed. We slept a lot, I think.

The milk tasted like chalk. At night, a terrible sound of iron doors closing; during the day, metal trays were emptied, then stacked. Then one day a woman who spoke our language was led in; they had taken her from her store, she said. She begged us to contact her family when we left; they didn't know where she was.

Mother refused to believe her, even though she repeated the same story over and over again, how you could be accused of Communism in nothing flat and then they kick you out, she said. She hoped we would take her letters. Mother knew she was lying, because this sort of thing never happens in America and most likely she was a policewoman trying to test us. I have often thought about that woman since, even though I don't remember her face in detail; she was thin, middle-aged, probably dead by now. She had spent most of her life in America; she spoke our language in a funny way. We didn't contact her family in New York; who knows if Mother mailed those letters. Even if we had tried to see her husband, it would have been impossible. Abruptly one day, they told us to pack, a car sped across New York once again; two men put us on a train for Chicago. Mother didn't believe that woman's story, but I don't know what she thought about this older man who showed up the day before we left. He told a similar tale — how he had been falsely accused of Communism so some men could get hold of his shop. They had him declared Communist and insane, but he was not crazy, he whispered to us and cried. He begged us to mail some letters. I have thought about him too later on because he was so scared somebody would see him giving us those letters; he was so frightened of the consequences he looked like a crazy person. I think we mailed them from Chicago.

Nobody believed me later, when I tried to tell them about this man and woman whose names I never learned. They were political prisoners who, after a time on the Island, were deported. With us it was different — X-rays taken and some questions asked (were you ever? have you been?), we were released. I still don't know why we were kept there for a week. It's all those parts you don't know that leave the mark; you question and wonder. It wasn't good that my first view of our new country is connected to barbed wire and prison. We were locked up every night. I worried about fire all the time, what if, what if. It wasn't good we came to the U.S. about the same time they killed Ethel and Julius.

Chapter Three

It must have been around the third day that we ventured outside, our address in my pocket. Except for a serious illness, this was the longest time the two of us had spent cooped up inside the house. We expected something good that day, an adventure, other kids, anything. At home in the summer we roamed up and down the creek and played everywhere on the entire street. We were lucky because our windows gave on to the garden, so you just jumped out if Mother screamed too much, and my aunt jumped out too to escape her suitors. In the summer we only came home to sleep. That's why we were so cooped up, so eager.

Still, it was funny they didn't try to prevent us. It was so unusual that she didn't worry the way she should have. They wanted us out, no doubt about it. If we lost that piece of paper with our address on it, nobody would find us in this city known for gangsters. It bothered me they didn't care enough. When we went to grandpa's in a village two hours away, she always left firm instructions about everything — what to do, what not; it bothered me that she broke the rule.

So here we were, alone, not sure what to do. To the right, the street ended by this place which had a red sign in the window and a stale odor of beer near the door. The window was large and dark but you could see men drinking inside, bent, faces invisible, their backs turned to us. In front of this place, red letters blinking BAR, where the street ended, dad's factory stood with its own street which didn't have a name. I didn't know the factory was so near. There was nothing to do but go in the opposite direction but it made no difference whatsoever, same patches of funny gray grass, more wooden houses like ours, some dogs then eventually a very large street with cars going full speed. The sign said, 'Chicago Boulevard.' This street extended forever in both directions, that's all. I wondered how people met each other without a market or a square; it didn't look like they had a street where you could promenade at night.

We got bored walking on that boulevard so we took a side street and got lost. I got so scared I was sweating all over until I remembered that the factory was to the right of the boulevard and that if we went toward it we would find our house, which was near that bar. I remembered our house also had a thin, sickly tree in front of it. All this reassured me. Then a man with very green eyes appeared in front of us. Using the only English words I knew I said, "Where is...?" unaware that everything else I said was in Serbian. He answered the same, "You're on it. This is one hundred twenty-third street, just keep walking. Your house must be in the next block." I wanted to say something, ask him where he was from but he walked away, a lunch pail swinging evenly in his hand.

Our adventure ended. Safe, not kidnapped, how happy they'll be, they must have worried to death about us. Going upstairs we heard again the howling of that dog then a drunk man appeared. They were both gray-looking, he and his dog. He said something to us and shut the door.

They were shouting at each other; then they stopped. We heard them. They said nothing to us or to each other for the rest of the day or it was more like mumbles. Her face was all red and puffy; he looked like a perfect stranger, which he was. The misery started right away, no doubt about it. If only we had not gone outside, we could have prevented it; they would not have dared in front of us. I blamed myself over and over again, 'if only' had a reality of its own, an imagined better version of our lives. Why did I blame myself so much?

It grew hotter still, the kind of heat we had never felt, no clouds anywhere, just this gray white sky. Under the roof of that wooden house we were unprotected — hot, so hot, humid too, and no trees anywhere in sight. Nobody slept and we tried wrapping ourselves in wet sheets which cooled us off temporarily. We stopped eating too, almost right away. The food had no taste, the milk which we had loved before and never had enough of, now tasted awful; even apples so beautiful to look at were no different from tomatoes, and they were like pumpkin inside. Stojan, who loved meat of any sort any time, and fought over it, even he was no longer interested because this new meat didn't taste like meat although the chickens looked so much better than our scrawny ones. Mother worried now that, if we continued like this, we'd die. She started adding more spices to everything, more garlic, more hot peppers, forgetting that it was already too hot. Then Stojan discovered pies in the grocery store, blueberry, cherry, apple, and he ate them the way you eat bread, a whole pie at once, but she let him do it. At least he was not losing weight as she and I were. Soon my clothes didn't fit any more and hers seemed very large.

She tried everything she could think of, that's for sure. She hung her lace curtains, the only pair we had brought with us, even though they looked out of place here, too white, too short, too lacy. We had known these curtains our whole lives because they were part of our Mother's trousseau, along with all those pillows, sheets, everything made with her own hands before her marriage when everything was very different and better and both she and our father were young. In the pictures of them, Dad is not Dad yet, he wears a white uniform with a dangling saber; she has a beret worn coquettishly to one side. They have so many wonderful friends, all young, handsome, laughing, the Adriatic is in the background and nobody is thinking yet about Stojan and me or the war which will soon come. You can tell they can't even imagine the war, Germans, bombs. Their faces in the pictures are not the ones we see now except once in a while when I remember, when I see Dad and me from around that time or soon after. He is racing with me on a sled, we run, we laugh, we fall. Not him now, before. Stojan can't remember that other person, the way Dad used to be once, for Stojan he'll always be this one, a grim factory-worker, silent, brooding, a man who didn't even know how to look at his son. He knew him less than me. Stojan didn't speak yet, that's why.

Mother kept trying, that's for sure, and now so many years later I can see that she was right when she said, you are lucky you had me, with him you wouldn't have survived. It's true. With him alone, we would have sunk. She made more lace and placed it wherever she could, lace with branches, leaves, her way of decorating, or replacing lilac, rose bushes under our window. That green sofa was so ugly. She hung her wash on the back porch but that she did just once — everything was covered with black dust, can you imagine. From then on, she did like everybody else, in the basement where the machine was. It was much easier here, the machine did the job, you didn't have to spend the whole day boiling and rinsing at the pump, and the bleach made everything really white. Yet — there is always yet — the sheets didn't smell of trees but of these basement smells, kerosene, gas, mold. She ironed them, regardless, folding everything in neat piles which went into the brown painted drawers that always stuck. She cursed those ugly drawers, "May the devil take them, may they rot!" She cursed him too. It was his fault. He only knew how to buy old junk. She would have never bought such ugly things, not her; to my mother her kitchen was more important than pretty dresses or a nice haircut.

Still, no matter what she did, the apartment looked dusty, we couldn't get over it. It made her angry. Our old place had clean pine floors you could eat from as the expression goes. Here, dust accumulated in the carpet, mixed with sweat and cooking smells, more dust on the window sills, on linoleum in the kitchen, and there was no point in airing the place. It only made it worse. The other home appeared now as a fairy tale, well-scrubbed, white-washed every year, a table of white pine, a wood stove with wood smells, white cupboards, white curtains, nothing extra. Not much garbage either. It was all simple, I had only a summer dress, and a winter dress, and a school uniform, and one good dress, a pair of winter shoes and a pair of sandals. The sheets and clothes were stored in the oak chests which smelled of quince and roses from the garden. We had no dust.

Dad decided to improve our lives, so he went and bought a fan and placed it on the table between the couch and that fat chair. Stojan sat in front of the fan immediately, with his pies, oblivious to everything, eyes empty, looking like some sort of round Asian god. The sound of that fan spinning is a guide to memory too. Don't touch it, he said. It could cut your hand off. I am still afraid of fans, the sound metallic, menacing, deathlike. Death is the reason why I never dared come near that time, afraid to remember it, afraid of what would happen to me if for a moment I crawl back inside her, that girl, that other me.

"Her dress is too short," somebody said about me. It had to be that man who drove us the first day from the station or maybe it was the woman who had her toenails painted in red who came just once and said that here girls wear longer dresses, as soon as childhood is over. In Chicago, childhood ended much earlier, around ten or so. So what was I? At home I was neither a child nor a girl yet; we have another word for those like me, kids who have the smallest breasts, tiniest hips, and have not been kissed yet. It's *devoychitsa* in Serbian. I was a diminutive of that word girl, which you became around seventeen or so but even then you couldn't wear lipstick at school or anywhere else. In the evenings the older girls did it, on the sly, and then it was only Vaseline of a strawberry shade, and they said they ate many berries, that's why their lips are so red. Here it was all different we noticed on the bus we took, all four of us. It was our first shopping adventure although we didn't know that word. Shopping as a pastime didn't even exist as an idea.

The bus was full of young girls. Mother said they have to be factory workers because she couldn't imagine students looking like these. They chewed something while talking, and then a pink bubble exploded in front of their mouths and they scooped up this mess with their fingers, threw it back inside their mouths, chewed on it some more and then that pink explosion all over again. Because of all the goo on their faces, we couldn't tell their ages at all, and they had plucked eyebrows and large hips, big asses, just about as big as older women at home. Girls as a rule were thin and none had skins like these, all sorts of pimples, covered yet protruding under that make up.

Their skirts fell to their ankles and appeared uncomfortable. You wondered how they managed to sit at all, with all those stiff white things under their skirts and a wire contraption everyone could see. All this took a lot of space on the bus, a whole other seat, but worst of all they looked so ill-at-ease, as if drowning. Now with all that extravagance and expansion at the bottom, below the waist, their blouses were tight-fitting and their breasts pointed out geometrically like very sharp mountain peaks. We didn't know they wore special bras which helped them achieve this effect and it made no difference if you had breasts or not. That must have been the reason why all those men talked about American breasts, how women take them off when going to bed and you just can't be sure that what you see, you'll get.

In addition to all this, the girls wore the strangest bulky white socks that even men at home wouldn't wear, and they made their legs or what was left of the leg very thick. Their shoes, flat with laces, in two tones, black and white, were the ugliest anyone had seen, if at least they were in one color, a uniform black or white, and we wondered why they didn't wear sandals in this heat. The total effect of their dress made you think of an umbrella upside down, and they slouched too when they stood up.

They laughed, looking at us. We were not to their taste either. At that moment on the bus we can't tell why they were snickering so much, later we did. It had to do with Mother's legs, all that black hair,

23

her armpits too. We didn't see their legs were shaved, it didn't even occur to us this was done because men liked hair on women where we came from.

Dad said to me on the bus, "You'll never wear those socks or those shoes, not my daughter, no blue jeans either as long as I am alive." Still, I needed some new clothes for this summer, all of us did. That was the reason why all four of us went on this expedition to a town a half hour away where there were people on the street and dancing music came from the stores. Mexicans, he said, they have pretty songs. They were a dark coppery color with shiny hair and eyes. I didn't know much about Mexicans, just that film with Marlon Brando.

We walked up and down the main street of Indiana Harbor, Dad leading the way. He finally picked one store because he liked the way it looked, empty and large on the other side of town away from the noise. He also liked the way they offered him a chair the moment we came inside. From this chair he watched me carefully as I emerged from the booth, and sometimes he said no, sometimes yes. He had definite tastes, blue was his favorite color, and he liked dresses of a simple cut. He settled on one of white foamy cotton, a pale blue one with a bolero jacket, and a navy silk which cost a lot. Father and I liked only the most expensive items, but it was not intentional, somehow our eyes and hands went toward those dresses which were the simplest in fabric and cut. It surprised us that it was so expensive, somehow we had imagined that the ruffles would cost more. How could we know that only the expensive stores do not list their prices in the window? I expected him to return everything but he said no. He liked everything we had picked.

Next we went shopping for bathing suits as if we were going on a cruise ship, as if we were not living in East Chicago, near the factory, and all this in a shop called Mademoiselle, a place we could not afford. Later we discovered you could buy all these things, dresses and whatnot for much less, except that none of my clothes later were as pretty as these. Bathing suits we had to have because we always had them and it was summer after all. This was an old habit, like going on a vacation, which people in East Chicago didn't do.

Dad had no vacation plans but he took this trip seriously; with a frown he dismissed this suit or that, he complained how thick, how unhealthy, not good to sit in a wet bathing suit for hours. There were wires in them at the top, too much fabric, all sorts of folds, and what is this skirt? he said. Fortunately there was a thin silky suit for real swimmers, and he said yes to this one. Now that I had a bathing suit, I had to have a pair of shorts, how else can you go on a vacation, and a blouse to go with it, a rubber cap for some reason to keep my hair dry. This was a pure invention, nobody ever had a rubber cap by the river, it must have been Esther Williams, maybe she wore a cap in the films we saw.

Mademoiselle had the cap but they didn't understand anything about rubber slippers, a protection against the sea urchins or sharp rocks, another fantasy on my part. Stojan and I walked barefoot in the summer over the rocks. Was this a make-believe demand, a replacement for the river and those rocks, what was it? Funny nobody said what seashore, what urchins or rocks? The saleslady only told dad and he translated that we would have to go to another shop for rubber slippers. We gave up on them since they were impossible to find.

In all this, Stojan was forgotten or his clothes appeared ordinary, just plain blue swim trunks, some long pants, a few shirts and socks. They were not spectacular-looking in color or shape, and Dad didn't watch him carefully, rejecting or approving each time. It got done, that's all, and you could tell Stojan was disappointed — my clothes took such a long time. Mother got the short end of it too — her dresses were not as pretty as mine but it wasn't anybody's fault that Mademoiselle had no clothes in her size and other stores had nothing she liked. She couldn't understand why she couldn't buy the same dress as mine just bigger. Even though she had lost a lot of weight, at Mademoiselle they said she was of a mature size, she needed a different store, and that meant dumpy ugly dresses in black or colors of mud. Mother was not fat but large, powerful- looking, with a bosom like Sophia Loren, a small waist, and hips that were more round than large. She had large bones, I guess the word solid would describe her body well.

That sea-blue wool dress, my spring jacket, and my burgundy red sandals were put away, later sent back home. Why didn't we keep those sandals with thick leather soles, made by my shoemaker, better than any I'd have later, why were they replaced immediately by white plastic ones called wedgies, with straps. You couldn't run in these and they made me walk funny, carefully, as if on ice. This was our attempt to be less noticeable, I guess.

Now that we had everything, we had no beach or any way to find one. Father had no car, and he hated them, along with all machines in general; machines he blamed for most things, wars, his job, his life. He didn't think it was necessary, walking is good for you, he said, and there is always a bus. We were not going anywhere. His shopping expedition had made him happy, as if he had taken a real trip, and besides his one-week paid vacation was over. Why only a week, we wondered, when at home they had one month, is this just for him or everyone? He couldn't explain why.

Mother did what she could. In the absence of anything else, she hung the icon of Saint Nicholas, our patron saint and protector, known to help sailors and homeless people. He was placed on the wall opposite the green sofa, next to the overstuffed chair and the fan. In front of him a candle flickered inside the glass just like at home for those special occasions in December and April and even though the flickering, the oil, the candle, and the saint were exactly the same, he looked out of place on this wall in East Chicago. You couldn't say why. It was as if he had lost parts of him during the travel, and we now had a copy, and knew it was a copy. For some reason the colors seemed faded, paler all of a sudden. He was no longer him, and I was not quite sure about me.

Chapter Four

Stojan and I drifted off to another world on the roof-top porch where Mother had tried to dry her sheets. It was not a real porch but a fire escape landing, covered by tar paper connecting Mother's bedroom with the back yard through a shaky staircase. The yard was not a yard either, just some dirt, that's all. Dad warned us right away, "The whole house could burn in ten minutes and these stupid wooden stairs in three. When in doubt," he lectured, "just jump." His reasoning was good, you could break your legs but you would survive. From that porch we saw the backs of houses like ours or smaller, patches of grass here and there, everything flat, extending forever then merging in the distance with the smoke from the factories on the South side. Sometimes the sound of an invisible train reached us, and I remembered our train, the day we left after the last whistle.

We gave in to the heat, we grew hypnotized by the sun, but once again we were together, Stojan and I. In the last couple of years we had stopped playing together, I had moved away from cops and rubbers, Tarzan and such, to my friends who were whispering daily about mysterious things only girls should know. He was younger than me. Now on this landing we were the same age or I became his or my girlhood stopped. Together, dazed by the heat, we drifted into a make-believe world created by both of us. Alone I couldn't have done it, alone I would have gone mad if madness is a prison of you and your thoughts unchecked, going in any direction. I started it, though. One day I said, "Imagine this, what if an airplane appeared, just imagine."

I don't know why I did it. Stojan loved the stories I used to tell him and his friends in the afternoons in front of our door. They were too lazy to read the books I'd read, preferring my retelling because they only wanted the action parts, who did what to whom, and then what. This time on the porch Stojan was different. Instead of waiting for my story to begin, he said, "Yes, I see it."

"Do you really?" I said surprised. Then I saw it too. The plane was flying very low trying to make up its mind. Did it see us?

"Sure," Stojan said, "right there, but where can it land?"

Stojan was smart, he could see that the yard was too small. The plane with its large beautiful wings was right above us. We waved.

"It doesn't have to land," I said, looking worried. "It could lower a special staircase, and we just climb on."

"Staircase?" he said, looking worried. "What's it made of?" "Rope," I said, "very strong rope, don't be afraid, I'll go first."

"No, you better go behind me," he said.

From that moment on, it was easy, although a bit scary on that staircase that suddenly just fell from the sky. It shook pretty badly as we climbed into the void, and I worried what if we fell, but nothing horrible happened and I managed to push Stojan inside, and after I got in they slammed the door. Everything was wonderful right away. The pilot, who had dark curls and looked like my aunt, grinned and said, "We couldn't come sooner. We got your message but the winds were very strong. You had nothing to worry about, you should have known that sooner or later, we'd rescue you. See, in the beginning your SOS was not loud enough."

"I didn't know we sent it," Stojan says.

"Of course we did, many times, and they only got the last one."

"On what?"

"On our minds, silly," I say convinced, and he accepts it, looking a bit puzzled. "I did it," I say. "I have a little switchboard in my head, I'll tell you all about it some day, we'll activate yours."

"That's good." he says.

So, in nothing flat with the sound of a plane overhead in real life, we travel back, drunk with happiness that's bigger than bliss. Bigger than anything in real life. There are no details that day on how we land, where, do they have to lower the staircase or what. We don't care to invent this. We are in such a hurry to think of details. And here we are. Everything is the same as before. Our garden is big, green, roses by the window, everything is exactly the same, every tree, the creek, all my friends, Stojan's old gang. Nobody asks any questions like tell us where you've been, nothing at all, it is as if we had just slept through a bad dream and now we woke up. What a relief. We never left. It must be true. That's why they don't ask any questions.

It's so good and so simple. We are at home. We actually believe this. Stojan resumes playing with forbidden slingshots, chasing chickens, and so on, and Mother doesn't stop him either because she too is so happy, she hums. I gaze at the rose bush and think about swimming later on, maybe I'll start a new book, or I'll stroll up and down the main street with Slava and Anka. The smell of summer is in me. My girlfriends whisper. Everything in sight hums gently. Soon, maybe tonight, my first kiss will happen, the interrupted one with the same boy who looks like a gypsy but is not really one. He has been looking at me for over a year. It's time. His eyes make me dizzy, it's better than going full speed on the sled, or spinning on the roller coaster. It can't be described really, it's the first time.

We went on and on about the return without getting bored at all. We continued it in the following days, I can't recollect how we managed to live the other part. Most likely we switched, the real life was just a bad dream and this other one on the porch was the one we ran to. Some details were changed by me, in a futile effort to prolong it. We enlarged part one, there were many enemy interferences on the waves, the reason my messages were not heard even though I shouted SOS, SOS. Then we had to find a new way to send them. Trick the enemy who was always faceless but listening to everything, including your thoughts. It took forever before the plane appeared. The plane was shot at, the weather grew stormy, big winds, snow, rain. Then I added tons of other kids who were being rescued just like us. Each one of them had his or her own story, of course, and their own attempts to break though the enemy waves. Some of our dreams we kept to ourselves — not that I knew what Stojan's were, and he didn't know about my stolen kiss, or the kiss that wasn't because he was not the right age to know such things. His friends snickered and whistled whenever a couple kissed on screen. So I left that part out and instead urged him to look at the snow, so big, so white, all the way up to our window in the morning when we wake up. "Look," I said, "it's still snowing."

He did. In front of us untouched snow extends all the way to the creek, the trees stand silent, branches moan from all that weight. Fast, we jump into our clothes, run out, lie on the top, make angels with our arms. The snow is so thick, it supports us. Silently softly angels get covered up. Lying like this, more snow falls into our mouths while we remain in the same spot without moving or sinking into the snow, our faces toward the sky.

Stojan gets up first, his face red. He throws a snowball at me, then says, "Let's go get the sled." The softness of the snow, the taste of it is on my tongue melting, the pain of it is so unbearable, the fear of it disappearing, do something fast, don't let it go, please don't go away yet, and Stojan looks so happy. I make a fast switch, "And the river," I say, "below that fall and we are barefoot."

"Yes", he says, looking so happy "at Grandpa's, under the mill."

That river is wonderful too, even though I had imagined the other one first. I don't mind. Under the mill, at Grandpa's, it's all white foam and then clear pebbles where our river rushes to meet another one. We drink the water, we drink the foam. We swim and swim; exhausted, we stretch out in the meadow by the river, the sound of bees all around us, butterflies are bigger than in real life. Cows and sheep stop to drink from the same river at the end of the day when the sun fades over the hill and soon all of us will sleep.

"Fireflies," Stojan says, "at night."

Right then, at that moment, it's all real, not much invented, home is still in our blood. There is nothing we can do, short of dying, not to think about it. We have to. It saves us. But there is always a moment I dread, when we have exhausted all of it, sucked dry every bit of snow, both rivers up and down, all the creeks, all the games, the plane has landed and instead of remaining there — we are still on this fire escape called a porch, black soot in the air, smelly tar paper under us. It's not snowing. At that moment when we can't think up more, either real or invented or anything —we are caught. I fear that part. Anything is better. In the heat of East Chicago my imagination then turns in the opposite direction, death, dying —jump, jump somebody whispers in my ear, you can always jump. Why not, why not, I hear my voice whisper back. I can always die. It's reassuring knowing it, my only certainty.

Underneath us, just below, our parents are arguing every moment they get. Their voices carry in a wooden house like this. Sundays are the worst.

Chapter Five

For the same reason she added more garlic, more pepper to our food, Mother decided we should go to church. It had nothing to do with religion but her need for people, her attempt to save herself and us. One of the peasants must have told her about it, it was not Dad's idea, he didn't care much for crowds or the church. So, once again we took the same bus for that town with the Mademoiselle store, and we wore our new clothes for this first social event.

A large group of men smoked and argued outside the church. It looked like the service was over except it wasn't. Inside a few men and more women stood on two different sides while kids fidgeted and cried. Fans buzzed. Women wore hats, a peculiar thing to do in such heat, and kids had too many clothes on, poor things. Poor me. Immediately I knew this was a waste of time — there were no girls or boys of my age, just some old people, hefty peasants in city clothes with their brats. In front of me a woman had squeezed her feet into a pair of high red heels, her legs were swollen and she wore gloves in this heat, black ones. And while I had liked peasants at home for many different reasons, these village immigrants wore tight dresses and suits and all that rouge, powder, lipstick on them struck me as misplaced.

An odor of incense mixed with armpits, in the heat I wondered if I was dreaming. Even the priest didn't seem like a priest, his face red glistening with a bushy black beard, and he had venom in his voice. As soon as he had finished his various chants, he switched to the other part, "Give money," he said. This was a way to fight Communism, he claimed. He passed a plate full of dollars and you were supposed to add to the pile. That other church near my school was cool, dark, mysterious, candles flickered, your feet echoed on the stone. You could go in any time you wanted to. I don't remember having to pay. Dad should have told us you had to. It was embarrassing to be so unprepared.

Leaving, near the door I noticed a picture of this guy with a long black beard and recognized him as one of the traitors from my school books. Here he was a hero, a candle burned under his picture. He was executed after the war for his deeds, helping the enemies of people and such, our teacher explained in the first grade.

Outside, men gathered around us. Dad, the center of attention looked both proud and uncomfortable. They were congratulating him, all those guys with big shoulders bursting out of their suits while he appeared even more fragile, short, his suit too large but of a much nicer cut, from London, dark gray with thin stripes. Then everybody moved to a large hall next to the church and soon men drank and argued like crazy and all I could do was watch.

This hall by the church was the place where they got married, where the funeral meals took place, and where they continued their obsessions every Sunday, politics and more politics, different positions on this or that, Balkan misery, all over with ages ago but not for them. When their lives stopped, around 41 or 44. It was boring, why would these men argue over and over again about events that couldn't be changed. It's over with, you wanted to tell them, stop. At home, nobody did anything as stupid as that because they were moving toward socialism and a better future. Our tomorrows will sing, my teachers said. With no enemies left, without any religion to divide, to confuse us, it was simple — we were just Yugoslavs. I was. Not these guys. They spoke

about betrayals and butchery in Croatia, all sorts of events we had
not studied at school and you couldn't decide whom they hated more:
Germans, Communists, or Croatian Fascists. I had never heard that
Croatian Fascists ran the horrible Jasenovac camp where thousands
died, children included. I preferred to think what my teacher said, that
the Germans did it all.

I noticed there were some differences among them — the ex-
German prisoners, who had skipped the war because they were locked
up in the camps had more gentle faces, melancholy eyes, while the other
ones who had fought the Communists and lost, appeared fierce, drank
more, got into fights which only confirmed everything my teachers said
about them. I couldn't really believe that I was watching all this, I, the
best pioneer in class was talking to men who used to kill with knives,
teachers said. Of course I didn't know all the facts, why, how, who was
right or wrong, I could only judge them by the way they acted in the
hall. Of course I said nothing. I was afraid of them. If Communists in
the books struck me as more rational, more orderly, and certainly more
optimistic, these men in Chicago were still a part of us, faces you saw
at weddings — when drunk with brandy they reached for the knife.
At home these bad elements were under control, there were fewer of
them. "Communism appeals to stupid idealists," Mother said once. Is
that me? Am I an idealist or an observer? What was she?

Then there were those like Dad who was neither this nor that, a
poor man who had sworn his loyalty to some king ages ago when he
was a cadet. That's what cadets had to do. I observed that these men
spoke to each other in the funniest way, "Mr. Major, Mr. Captain,
Your Honor," they said and here they were working in the mills, or
doing jobs their domestics had once done. Communism simply
reversed things, their servants took power, and they got their servants
jobs. That's how I viewed their situation, and what's more this reversal
struck me as just, I mean, why should the same families, or the same
few always have the good times?

A few younger men, or at least not terribly old, maybe thirty-five or so, too old for me, looked so sad as they drank. Their fiery songs took them into the future when they'd take over, Communists would run and they'd marry the girls they left behind. Dad said in a half-whisper, "What rubbish, not a chance, they'll never go back, or marry, they'll just stay here and rot." That's how he talked, always statements of this sort, just gloom and more gloom and no chance for escape. I'll escape or die, I kept thinking. The question was how.

In the midst of all this, the peasants continued to be the same as the ones we had met the first day — more talk about their cows, their fields, and their fear they'll never see them again. And then nobody will ever visit their graves. They compared their cows, how much milk the spotted one gave, forgetting, poor guys, that 'the spotted one' or 'the blackie' had to be, must be, dead. You wanted to shake them and tell them wait a minute. Peasants never spoke about fighting Communism and such or what positions they'll have after the takeover, whom to kill first, whom to spare. They couldn't care less. They remained consistent in their grief over those cows, and because it was a true love I felt bad thinking about Grandpa's mill, the white foam, and the smell of grass in July. I could never describe that smell nor find it again because it was everything else — the wooden bridge, the sheep with the bells, a peasant leading a horse, women naked, laughing, washing the clothes and themselves — all this was included in that smell of grass. That's why I felt bad for those peasants and me. And I observed us feeling invisible, like a fly on the wall. It was better to observe than not to, it was a way out, it was something.

Dad didn't fit into any of these groups, that's why his loneliness was the biggest. He didn't walk or talk like some of those officers who pretended, can you imagine, they were still at some military ball. He couldn't cheat. He had given up on everything, even on the king and queen, titles, and all that make-believe. He said, "So stupid, so dumb, that would-be major you met, he works in my factory, what sort of major is that, he'll never go home, all of them are just a bunch of liars and pretend people, and the king is the biggest crook of them all." All this left him unprotected, without a dream or make-believe and the present was what it was, and in it he couldn't enjoy what he had, what others wished for — us. "What a lucky man," others said to him, "not a lone wolf like us." This didn't impress him. He remained who he was, unchanged by his good fortune. Maybe he was stuck too, just like them, and couldn't advance from that short-lived time, the only one when everything was good — he was a young father and husband and the future was still to come. Then the war destroyed everything, our house, his world, Mama was no longer young, and we were grown up. Having skipped all sorts of steps, he didn't know how to behave with us. At least I was lucky, I remembered him occasionally the way he really was, laughing in the snow with the sled speeding, just the two of us. He remembered me too at four or five and tried to do what he did then, tickle tickle then a chase around the table, come sit on my lap he said. He couldn't see I was not five.

When they argue, and she calls him names, I try to keep him the way he was then, my dad, the one I had been missing all those years. I wouldn't miss a dreadful person, would I, could I? He was not that way before. Now there is not much left of my father in East Chicago and maybe there won't be much left of us, I thought with dread. Maybe it's the air and all this dust, maybe I too won't remember the way I was. My dad was calm and sweet and kids clustered around him because he loved them. Everybody said that, even my Mother, no, I didn't invent it, all of them said what a wonderful father he was. This dad, the one here, who lost everything and himself— is all different, half-angry, half-sad or not there. He only likes dictionaries, English, French, German, he seems to enjoy looking up words. "Italian is so beautiful," he says, "even if you curse someone it doesn't sound like a curse. You should learn Italian, don't bother with German." He spoke German but I am not tempted, the sound of German is rough, like 'achtung', like commands, like dog barks and then I remember Partisan girls swaying from the trees in the square. An old, very old memory. Blue

36

faces swollen, don't look, don't look, cover her eyes, they said. I looked anyway. I saw them. Germans were in my first grade books too, with pictures of dogs, Nazis, and ways to recognize a grenade.

Dad had left so many books at home, I've read all of them at least once. A Thousand and One Nights had pictures in silver and gold and violet shades, all sorts of travel books with pictures of the Sudan, Zanzibar, and Bali, where everyone seemed happy and girls swam naked then ate fruit. There were medical books and books about improving health care among the peasants and many novels about people who are always unhappy in love. I knew nothing about love, love is just a word and no more, I only wished I had brought some of those books along, but she didn't let me take even the ones that were my awards for excellent grades every year, with the teacher's signature in front. We took no books, there was no room for them. We could only have two suitcases for three of us, and then I don't think it mattered that much to her because she always said, "Stop peering in that damn book or you'll go blind." I should have snuck a few, I should have.

Father peers at dictionaries any chance he gets. "It's hopeless," he says, "there is nobody to practice with." In the factory nobody talks, and in addition English is so illogical he says. His big dream was to prove it with a book he would write, he always got angry about the spelling of English words. Spelling is a new word, a new idea for us. Stupid, stupid, he says, why should this word 'thought' have seven letters instead of three. 'Tot.' The sound of 'th' is hard for us; he says 't' instead and he says V instead of 'w' which is also impossible. And why should difficult have two Fs when one is good enough, and why should three be written with two 'e's for example. Dumb, so dumb. Why didn't they simplify their writing the way we had done it in the nineteenth century so you could write exactly the way you speak.

Even though he said 't' instead of 'th', he spoke better than other people around us, that is he could read a paper and understand what they said on the street. For that reason, all those peasants came over so he could write things for them with the gold pen from England, every letter perfect, in blue ink. They were either official letters, problems, inquiries in English, or personal ones in our tongue, which began in the same way, "My dear ones, my sorrows, my lambs, I am fine and hope you are healthy, God willing. Did it rain enough, I worry about the wheat."

He wrote exactly what they said then he read it to them. Sometimes they wanted extra thoughts added like "If I were you I would plant corn this year" or they would say, "Scratch that part about my accident in the mill," and Dad would get angry because the page would look bad. They cried often and it looked so sad, men with big shoulders crying in the kitchen just like kids. Our sad destiny, they said. At the door, they always tried to give him some money, which he refused every time and they refused to leave until they had left these carefully folded dollars in Stojan's hands and mine.

That's how Dad was, not the kind of person who would know how to take advantage of anyone, Mother said, and what's more even a blind man could take him for a ride. Her words were confusing, just as you thought she had something good to say about him, in the same breath she had to add the second part.

All in all, he must have been too lonely and because of that he fell under the influence of this man he had known for a long time. They had been prisoners together. He was the man who drove us that first day from the train station, but it turned out that the same man had advised him not to send for us and at the worst moment when we were ready to leave and everything was sold. Who knows why. Mother said he was after Dad's money except he had none. Out with that one. Most likely he was afraid that their friendship would change once we arrived. They were lonely together for so many years. That day at the train station we were too stunned to pay attention to him but even if we had nobody could ever imagine that Dad had a friend who was completely nuts. We discovered it bit by bit. He was silent that day. He was hiding.

The next time he came to our place, this man only lectured, what to do, what not, his fingers raised. Looking at me, he said, "She must wear her hair braided, and go to church every week." We laughed, all three of us, he spoke like an actor in a nineteenth century play. He got angry next, his face turned bright red. "You laugh when you should be careful. You are not careful enough. I know things."

"Don't meander," Mother said. "What do you know?"

"If anyone asks if you love America," he whispered, "you better say yes, yes, I do. If not, they punish you. They have their spies."

"Birds ate his brain," Mother said after he left. "Where did you find him of all people?" Father began defending him, she snickered, and that got them going on a new argument, a big fight, a war, and they tried to destroy each other's friends and each other with terrible words. Always on Sunday. You wished Sundays would not occur.

Another Sunday, the same guy appears, and the first thing he says coming through the door is this, "You can tell immediately that there is no discipline or strong leadership in this house. The air smells of insubordination, mark my words." We laughed and laughed again, and he was funny-looking too, with a very pale face, sunken eyes, and that wild red hair you don't see in our people. He looked like a Russian nobleman gone to seed, someone out of The Brothers Karamazov, my last book. Sad to think about it, that word last.

When he left, Dad was silent for a long time; then he said, "See, even he can tell right away there is no discipline here." This guy probably told him all sorts of things when they were alone, how Dad is no longer in charge of his troops. Dad was under his influence for sure, maybe his madness appealed to him, maybe they were both mad. Dad would repeat everything the crazy guy said, he thought about it, you could tell he did.

Later, much later, it turned out he was the one who wrote to the FBI and the immigration office to accuse Mother and me of Communism.

Stojan was skipped. For some reason this didn't surprise us, you could expect anything from a crazy person, but we didn't expect the FBI to take these letters seriously and from a man who later ended up in a mental institution. But that didn't happen yet, will not happen in this book.

Chapter Six

We are in a room without a window. June has passed. It must be July. We are in a brick building called Roosevelt High and ours is a special class, just for Stojan and me. Somebody took us there, Father most likely. On a steel table so large it occupies half of that room, a machine makes sounds we are supposed to repeat. We had never seen a machine like this. They call it a tape recorder. It's not an easy word.

"I am Mr. Smith, you are Mrs. Jones", the voice of a dead person comes out of that machine.

"How do you do, Mrs. Jones. Fine, thank you."

"I am Mr. Smith. I am a man. I have a hat on. My hair is blond."

"I am Mrs. Jones. I am a lady. My dress is white. My hair is brown. It's a nice day today, Mr. Smith."

Their voices taste of steel and stale air. Mrs. Jones talks more than Mr. Smith. We watch the book to see what they do and how they behave and then we repeat just like them. "How do you do" sounds strange. Do they really say it every time? "Fine" is even weirder when I look it up in the dictionary. Our parents would never say fine if you asked them how do you do, nor would anyone I know say fine, thank you. They would say all sorts of things, good and bad, but it wouldn't be just fine. To say just fine would be too cold, too stingy. At home they'd think you were hiding something, maybe a terrible disease.

The boredom of it. We repeat the entire morning, we listen, repeat like parrots some more, we grow sleepy, yet this machine continues on and on because this bald man comes in to make sure. Then the machine went crazy somewhere in the middle of the week, Mr. Smith and Mrs. Jones accelerated their speech, and we got scared of some unnamed disaster. We unplugged the damned thing, what else could you do? Unfortunately, it wasn't dead. The same bald guy in the gray suit fixed it, smiling at us all along, pronouncing each word slowly, the way you teach a two-year-old. He believed we could understand him if he spoke this way. His name was Simon. He was a principal. He had the same voice as Mr. Smith.

At noon, it was over. We walked back along that big boulevard, dizzy from the heat and that machine. Fine thank you, can't get Mrs. Jones out of my head, how do you do, my hair is blond. Fine thank you. Three hours of it, how do you do. Around us, walking in the same direction, kids like us carried books in their arms, a strange American custom, why didn't they get a school bag to keep their books and papers clean. I regretted having left my old leather one behind, with my initials, the one Mother bought me in the first grade. Dad said Americans are practical but why did they carry those books against their chest, and what were they doing in school in July? Dad had no answer. We were alarmed, maybe they don't have summer vacations here, maybe we'll go to school all the time. Scary. I loved school but I loved summers as much, bare feet, climbing trees, long lazy days, all those things our teachers said were good for you and every child should have.

She waited for us, ready with lamb, liver, soup, sweets; she baked now every day, worried about the weight loss which meant bad things, bad, TB, God forbid, knock on wood, spit three times. She feared illness all the time, especially when Father said, you'd better not get sick, here doctors are not free, and then we heard horror stories about hospitals refusing you if you can't pay. Mother's aim was simple — she had to save us, and if we looked plump, we were not sick. We were alone again, the three of us, except when Father worked the night shift but then he slept most of the day recovering.

He didn't worry about food or our health, or at least he didn't say so. He worked in a place he described as hell, flames, terrible heat, grinding machines. To rest from misery, sometimes when he didn't work in the evenings he went downstairs to see wrestling on a television set, and we went with him a few times. We had nothing else to do. But there was a problem. In addition to a TV set, our compatriot on the first floor also had an unusually ugly wife whose washing machine Mother had to use the first weeks. Mother hated her and the machine, and she said she did. Dad was not very social, if anything he did everything to avoid people, but he took wrestling seriously and then he got hooked on it. He was so serious about details nobody could say a word. On TV, men grunted, threw each other with rage, sat on each other's backs, it looked like they were going to break each other's arms, and yet they bounced off the floor like rubber balls. Dad and this other man shouted, made bets on the winner; they had their favorites who looked the same, disgusting, fat with ugly muscles and no neck. It was unpleasant. Of course, we didn't get involved and that German woman said nothing, just stared ahead looking like a hound dog. Her face was something, with large red freckles, upper teeth that stuck out even when she had her mouth shut, carrot hair, and two small dead eyes. We would not have paid attention to her face if she had been a more pleasant person but she didn't even look at us once. Mother's dislike of her was justified. So, it was a great relief, an improvement, when Father gave in and got his own 'brain-washing machine' of a medium size. For a man who had hated television with a passion he suddenly argued that all of us would learn English faster, he just couldn't admit he was hooked on wrestling. It would have been beneath him. And he didn't know nor did we that it was all rigged, the winners and the game.

That July went like this — after three hours with Mr. Smith and Mrs. Jones and that bald guy who demonstrated the sound of th by sticking his tongue out and spitting at us, relief with pork chops, lamb chops for lunch, then Gene Autrey, the Lone Ranger and gun pursuits on TV. In between the shootings, there was something new — commercials it was called. We took them seriously, why would they lie? And it wouldn't be permitted, Mother said. Mother believed everything Radio Free America said about America, it matched her own dreams, good and bad. On TV, toothpaste fought tooth decay, sprays killed germs which were as big as mice, you had to be equipped for a fight at all times. Everywhere you turned the world was full of dangers, diseases lurked, you had to clean and clean to kill the hidden enemies with bleach. You win temporarily, and the world is safe and oh so white. White was the favorite color in America I decided because they scrubbed and scrubbed and bleached, clothes, face, teeth. They were scared of dirt, we thought watching those commercials, they couldn't stand the smell of armpits or any other way people smelled. I didn't know before this was a serious problem; I liked the way my mother smelled, and I liked the smell of her armpits. No, we never used deodorants, we didn't have them, although Mother said she had used them before the war but it wasn't good for you, it made your skin itch. On TV everyone smelled bad and people didn't like you until you used this stick: then they hugged you and said mmmm. Both men and women smelled bad except that girls washed their hair more, all the time, and scrubbed their faces with brushes while men smoked while galloping on horses in the west or they swam and then smoked, a Coke in their hands on a white beach. Each puff of smoke looked like ecstasy, better than anything, so free — you, the horse, and the smoke. That's how you relax, a new word. You gallop next, so free, still smoking, puffing away, clouds around you, each guy on the horse another John Wayne. I liked the white beaches the best and the restaurant this couple goes to, soft music, the ocean on one side. Then everything gets interrupted when she sees dandruff on his shirt.

How can you tell which soap is better if each one says it is, Palmolive, Camay, Lux and what about shampoos which we had never used before because you didn't need them and why wash every day? My hair was washed separately with the rain water stored for that purpose, and then Grandmother rinsed it with the herb tea, maybe once a week maybe once in two. Why wash it more, why every day, I didn't smell, or maybe I did but didn't notice it. I had never thought about people smelling bad, was I used to the bad smells without knowing it? It was amazing daily. Commercials were more interesting than the films they interrupted, they were short, fast, and they told you how to live and what to do. If a kid fell down and scraped his knees, parents hugged and kissed the kid right away, then everything ended well with a band-aid. Buy band-aids in a box, buy two, be safe! We couldn't get over this, Stojan and I. At home you didn't mention your bruises, it was best to hide them or you would hear all those horrible laments, 'Look what you did again, you'll be the death of me, look what you did to your new pants.' We told Mother to watch carefully the band aid stories, in America that's how she should behave. No more screaming, just kisses and hugs. Dad put an end to our illusions about commercials when he said, "Lies and more lies, they are just urging you to get more shit, and what's more it can have very dangerous consequences. Unless you are careful your brain will turn into toothpaste or rot." He shouted, "Close your eyes when the commercial comes on, pretend you don't hear it." He claimed it was better propaganda than anything Hitler had invented and that was sufficient reason for Mother and him to fight all over again because she couldn't stand comparisons with Hitler and because she, more than the rest of us, wanted to believe in America. This belief took her through everything, the Vietnam war, and the civil rights movement, and Iran Contra, and it was only in '92 with the civil war in Yugoslavia that she lost her old dream about America when she saw that the TV didn't always tell the truth. I have never bought a single product they advertise on TV, then or now. Dad's influence or what?

Stojan sat in front of the set, eyes glazed, hardly blinking. I couldn't develop any real passion or even a bit of surprise for this new machine with boring pursuits and guns. The commercials made it impossible for me to get involved, I also missed the darkness of the movie houses, the separation between real life and the screen, the conversations afterwards. If you could get up to get a glass of water, it's not the same thing. The TV remained a piece a furniture, a bulky one on which Mother placed her lace doily, just like she did on the sofa and chairs. It was a gadget with images which were less interesting than stories told, less real than books. Even the circus was much better, men ate fire, women danced on the high wire and people laughed when a bear appeared to the sound of a drum. At home. This was far away yet more real than TV or our apartment, the only real life was the one before, the one I was afraid to lose. I worried it might leave me, not about commercials which bounced off me without penetrating. Alone, at night, I tried to keep, to save the river, our sled, our old creek. I had to do it alone, Stojan didn't want to come along any more, and who can blame him — this machine was more exciting than our sad stories which had nowhere to go and the ending couldn't change. "That plane will never come," he said one day and I knew I had lost him.

Dad argued with the TV as if it were a person. He muttered, he screamed, abruptly he stood in front of it, then he killed it with real joy. "There," he said, turning it off, "now you can't blab any more and tell lies." The Saturday bandstand matinees provoked him too, savages, he shouted at those boys and girls who shook their arms and moved their feet while everything else, their faces, their shoulders and hips, remained frozen. They didn't upset me at all. I watched them with the distance of an anthropologist observing a rain dance, I only wished they were more handsome to look at. Boys' hair was either short, thin, cut so it stood up, or it fell onto the forehead in one single greasy wave. Their clothes were as unattractive as they were, those ugly white socks, baggy pants which risked falling down, everything clumsy including the two toned shoes, my luck to fall among such people, if only we had gone to Bali. I loved the way everybody looked in Bali in my old books, they swam in clear rivers without bathing suits.

"You call that dancing!" Dad said, furious as the kids shook and rocked on TV. His rage pushed him to show me what real dancing is like, something he knew how to do. "This is how you waltz," he said with a sweeping arm movements, "tango is like this and in the foxtrot you..." he demonstrated around the kitchen table with me as his partner. "But," he raised his voice, "you can't just get up and drag some woman with you on the floor, you have to know how to invite a lady to a dance." He bowed slightly for this, one arm bent at the waist, the other one extended, the way a ballerina thanks her audience at the very end. "May I have this dance?" he asked and I said yes. My part was simpler if I said yes. He never told me what to do if I don't feel like it, do I just say no or what, or do I say no, not now, later.

"I don't remember you dancing before," Mother said, looking at us. Her face was red, she had tears in her eyes. You couldn't tell if she wanted to laugh or cry.

You couldn't really figure him out, what he really liked, what he was opposed to. Just as we had decided that he hated everything modern, artificial, American, he would surprise us. He told me I could curl my eyelashes upward with this little instrument he had seen in some woman's magazine. Your lashes look bigger this way. If I wanted it, he said he would get it for me. No, I told him, I didn't like the way those turned up lashes looked, and he seemed disappointed. I was disappointed in him, because he was not consistent in his outlook. He was less admirable now and all because of that stupid lash-curler which he discovered in Mademoiselle while trying to learn new words.

He bought, then studied True Romance, Screen, magazines with pictures. He underlined the new expressions in red ink. But if he was able to push TV away as lies and fraud, he didn't expect the same thing to exist in print so with new words he also accumulated all sorts of beauty tricks, how, what to do with creams. He took the printed words seriously. Then we saw him or she saw him for the first time. It bothered her more than me. I had seen him before, he did it in front of me, but she was shocked that day I think. "He's gone crazy, God help us," she whispered to me.

Dad was standing in front of the mirror rolling his eyes, baring his teeth like a wolf, pouting as if for a kiss. She crossed herself then laughed and laughed until she shook all over. He did look funny. He didn't know he was being observed.

He told her quietly her laughter was foolish. This is how you stay young but some people don't care nor are they interested in improving their skins or their minds. This got them into an immediate fight, an all-out war, an uneven struggle because he could only do small stabs, she gave it to him with bombs.

"Real men," she lectured as if for thousands, "do not prance like fools in front of a mirror." Her real men were always tall and dark, handsome and strong, but on the fierce side. They rode horses, guns in one hand, and their horses were as wild as they were. I don't think she had ever known anyone like that except in our history books when all those men rose against the Turks, but at least she didn't expect a man to look at himself in the mirror so much. She thought it was a ridiculous pastime for women, too.

He told her she was ignorant. She didn't read the magazines or she would know that beauty is not accidental, nor good teeth and "If rose bushes need to be pruned," he said, "why then, I ask you, shouldn't we?"

"Are you comparing yourself to a rose?" Mother laughed a mean laugh and then of course he had to jab her, and then she said, "What about your scarecrow friend, go prune that ugly bush." That was a reference to Dad's friend, the crazy guy with red hair who came less and less, then stopped coming. There was nothing you could do with him, he didn't even appreciate Mother's good food. Others continued, one more than the others, a handsome peasant with a gold tooth whose favorite cow Lenka gave at least twenty liters of milk. This day he stopped their bickering when he knocked on the door. Maybe they continued without us but at least we were not there because this man took us to movies for the first time, in the center of East Chicago where Chicago Boulevard intersects another large street.

This was like downtown at home, although there were not that many people on the street. In a restaurant with large windows we saw men and women perched on stools. They drank milk with a straw and ate with their mouths open but nobody spoke to each other. They looked so lonely through the window or maybe I was lonely looking at them. We passed by many stores, clothing stores, a store with guns, bars, dark inside with red signs in front blinking bar, bar. Not far from all this there were railroad tracks, right in the center of town, a strange sight for us. The trains were all freight and very long. They didn't stop here but passed through, rushing toward better places, Santa Fe, Pacific written on the cars. The passenger train was further away but there was no real train station, and it's a problem when it rains, the man who took us to movies said. He didn't have a car, but he had a bike.

He was handsome and must have known it, a little bit. We liked him because everything about him was even — his glance, his smile, his perfect teeth except for that gold one. He held himself straight, head slightly to one side, just like in his photos; somebody must have told him he looked good this way. Mother appreciated his clean white shirts, dad said he was a nice man but you couldn't talk to him about anything, I liked him because he didn't talk too much. I imagined him as a wonderful father for some reason, he would gaze and smile and never scream. His name was Ivan but I remember him as the peasant with the gold tooth.

That July he said you could go inside the movie house any time, in the middle, at the end, you could stay as long as you wish, even see the film again. Amazing! And there were no lines, no fighting for tickets. But first we had to be prepared, he said; in America people eat while watching the film, in order to save time. He said that's the most important thing in America, time is money and money is honey but he

49

couldn't explain more being uneducated. What were they saving time for I wondered, time didn't exist before, or if it did it was some other time, morning, noon, spring, fall. Once again he only shrugged and left us to shop so we could see a movie just like the Americans — with food.

He came back with fried chicken legs, ham, bread, peaches, and we ate all this slowly in an empty house which had a strong odor of butter and old sweat, and it looked like a cave. However, it was wonderfully cool, and on the screen it was snowing too. The film was called 'White Christmas' and everyone in it looked happy. It snowed and snowed throughout the film and all those people kept singing how they dream about Christmas even though they had it. The entire world was white and pink and their faces were pink too, big smiles, white teeth. I couldn't stand it. It bothered me we had been lied to, duped because that's how we saw America at home, on film, all pastel shades, or deep blue of the swimming pools. None of those films were made in East Chicago. If only we had known.

Outside, on the street, we were overwhelmed by the heat of the sun. I remember: it was July, asphalt glistened, smoke rose from the mills in the distance, then the sudden thunder of a freight train going over the tracks.

Chapter Seven

They were shouting at each other when we got back from school even though it was not a Sunday. They didn't hide it from us. That was a bad sign. The war had started for real. And the revelations happened, bit by bit, the reason for her red eyes and all the bickering. Because she could not imagine my own misery or imagine kids unhappy she revealed hers to us. Maybe she had to do what she would not do at home where a neighbor would have heard it, she had to tell someone, I guess, even though I wished it otherwise. It was horrible — he, always referred to as he, him from then on, had showed her a picture of a German woman he had known in some camp or after the camp. Imagine, Mother said, just imagine him sleeping with the enemy while we starved, while they killed us and bombed us. She could forgive him this ugly slut but not his words, never! He told her (pure madness on his part) — he said that she was not attractive any more. He dared talk about wrinkles to a woman who had a high opinion of her looks, who had rescued her kids with her own hands from the ruins and then worked day and night to feed us. All this was true, my mother was both attractive and heroic, and everybody including herself thought so.

It was unforgivable and stupid, why did he do it, he didn't have to. She, on the other hand, didn't have the necessary distance (how could she after all?) to understand that he didn't see the bombed house nor her struggle, nor could he imagine it, his head full of his own horrors after he left us. They were locked into their pasts that couldn't be shared, and then their views on life were different too, I noticed right away. Dad had absorbed some western ideas, while hers remained old style, out of the epic songs, children before anything, you save them first, you live for them, make sure they grow up, a man honors and respects his wife because she is a mother, the most sacred position of all. There was no doubt in her mind about this, no gray areas, it was absolute, it couldn't be discussed.

And there was more. With each breath worse and worse. He told her (while we were in school or while we took walks) how she had neglected herself, her skin, her hands, her hair, as if she had money or time for perfect nails and creams. All true. She worked all the time, poor Mama, poor us listening to her. Then, as if all this was not enough, he asked, she said, can you imagine, "Did you have lovers too?" The question alone was sufficient, the nerve to suggest, to even hint about her reputation. My mother's reputation was as good as gold, of course it was, not that I understand really what she means by that word. When she recovered from the shock and gathered enough strength to tell him, how can you even think about it, of course not, he said, "Well, it's because nobody wanted you, or you would have had them." Those lovers. He dared tell her all this, to a woman known as a hero, a fighter by the entire town where hundreds of men wanted to marry her, what a fool she was. I wished she had done it, we wouldn't have left. I say nothing. It's too late now. What's a lover like? I wonder.

She was red in the face, her eyes red too, she couldn't stop, same story over and over again but a bit differently each time. We are in the kitchen; he has gone to work. "I could have had anyone, there was Marko, Mirko, and Jovan, but I never gave up on him, we were a family, we had to get reunited. Do you think I would do anything to cast a shadow over my reputation and yours?" she turns to me, "So your fiancé says when your time comes, 'No, I can't marry the girl whose mother is a slut.' "

I wish she wouldn't include me in their misery. Who are Marko, Mirko, and Jovan, do I know them? Did she invent them?

"Don't look at me that way," she says, "good family is the most important thing when men look for a wife. People pay attention to such things." What wife, I kept thinking, I wasn't even kissed. And then it ends up being my fault, why she didn't have the lovers she wanted to. To me even that word lover is strange, unknown, without reference to real life; she never talked about lovers before, nor did anyone. I am fifteen, I wished I had kissed someone. I wish she had all those lovers, Mirko and Jovan, I would have given her my permission. I would have said go out with Marco, go kiss him if you wish, go sleep with him too. I don't really understand that word sleep, sleep is sleep for me, what's the big deal.

Lost, numbed by the heat, I wasn't sure if she was telling us the truth, because she had a gift for exaggeration, a flamboyant oratorical style combined with a gift for mimicking just about everyone. She could do five or six people, like a play, going back and forth. I wanted to be fair to both sides at war, but how can you know who really said the first thing, who fired the first shot. In other words, did he start with the wrinkles and a picture of that monster or did Mother say something nasty to him first? Before I could judge accurately, I had to know the truth and that meant he should tell his side of the story. He should have been right there to defend himself, I didn't think it was fair for her or anyone to come to some conclusion without the other party.

He was silent often while she had a horrible temper, real explosions when she was angry, so it made sense that she fired first but then you just don't know. Maybe he made her angry without saying a word. I wanted to be just, get all the facts before the verdict while she only wanted me to be on her side. And that I couldn't do. She wanted me to comfort her, console her as always, but who had ever consoled me? Grandma had. I said nothing. There was nothing to say. "Wrinkles, wrinkles," she kept shouting as a new wave of anger swept over her, wounded to the core. Yes, it must have hurt terribly, I think now, as a grown-up, older than she was that day in the kitchen, of course it did, feeling for her what I couldn't then, me at fifteen. My sympathy went to him, as the weaker party, and I was like him silent, unable to shout, fight, or look for some other relief.

She had fought many wars in her life, she was strong, tough in every way including her body, her large bones. Mine were small like his, and I was fair like him — another sign of my weakness, she often said. I was weak. To make sure we didn't weaken and switch to his side, not even a tiny bit, for she suspected me capable of such treason — she went further. A few days later, with him away, she sat us at the kitchen table once again and told us in a very solemn way what nobody knew before, not a single person except our aunt, what most likely she wouldn't have ever told us if everything had been right or if we had stayed at home — she weakened briefly or she lost control or maybe not — she said she had been married before.

For me, the sensation of ground shifting, just like the day the house was bombed or something like it. Where am I? Who is she? Through the windows nothing is real, houses are a blur of gray, a month has passed, but maybe it's more, maybe it's been years, maybe she'll tell us next we are not hers. Once you start, you can't stop, there is no end to it. Nothing is real, not even my hands. I imagined her capable of anything, I didn't look like her, and if you examined him feature by feature, I didn't resemble him either. There you have it — they found me, what else?

After a long silence, and our initial shock, she told her story, or what she called her tragedy. It happened like this — they married her off at sixteen by force (why, how come, where) to a horrible man who was crazy, sick, and cruel, and then — we gasped — she had a child with him. I had a brother, another one! That proved I was perfectly right to imagine all sorts of things, where will she take us next, what will she choose to tell us, what not? With her, you could never be sure. The story continued — she leaves the baby, she escapes one day over the high mountains, rivers, and lakes; her feet bleed, rocks are sharp, the ground full of snakes; then finally she reaches the sea where Grandma had a restaurant in Dubrovnik by the port. (This grandma whom I loved more than anyone was not a real grandma although we called her that; she was Mother's aunt who had never married and preferred to live with us). Suddenly I began wondering about her too, what else is there, who is she really? It was unheard of at that time for a woman to have a restaurant.

"What about my brother?" I ask, having gotten attached to him already. I can hardly wait to meet him, what will he look like? Why didn't she tell us this before?

"He was killed by the Germans," she said, "with his uncles. Nobody knows their graves. He would be a grown man now," she says.

I imagined him unbearably handsome, with dark curls, like Saint George, and like my favorite Partisan hero, the one who threw a bomb at the German tank. He was dead too, and my brother didn't live long, and there was a reason why we hated Germans that much. And that woman downstairs who looks like a hound dog is German and so is Dad's slut in the picture he had showed her. He had to be crazy to show her the picture.

She had us. Stojan who never cried for reasons that were unrelated to himself, cried now, his face red. His tears just kept coming and he didn't bother to wipe them away. The tears on his baby face were worse than anybody's, sadder than my own, but at that moment we are united, the three of us, by her sad life and our loss. One moment I had a brother, the next second I had lost him. Somewhere in the mountains in Hercegovina, a region I didn't know, although I would have gone the following year on the class trip. I've never seen her home town either, too bad we didn't go there at least once. She had us that day because she told this story differently from all the other ones, in a low voice, whispering, as if choking in pain, and she looked like Stojan's sister, and I was her mother or grandmother or an older aunt. She had trained me to sit, to listen, to console — something she herself could not do.

At that moment her pain appeared so much greater than mine, my own paled, shrank. She was the way she was because nobody cared for or worried about female children where she came from, not her mother or her mother's mother in a warrior's tribe which valued only the sons. The sons died all the time either fighting each other or the invader. With me the line was broken, I had Grandma and Dad and all my neighbors. And I was born under socialism, not in the dark ages. Nobody would force me to get married, like her, like her mother. A part of me knows she was a better mother than her own; she didn't have ten children, but two. She didn't go to school. She made sure I went, and I have read many books, the reason why I aim for clarity rather than outbursts. (Read and read and read, my teachers said, read for no reason, the more you know, the richer you are, said the posters on the wall.)

I am glad she told us, a clue for all the things she couldn't be. It's better than not knowing.

As she cries, I remember vaguely that time long ago after the war when she received some letter and then cried for days and Grandma cooked her herbs to make her forget. Up to that letter, she didn't know, I suppose, who was alive, who not; the roads were cut, and in addition to Germans we had a civil war. She didn't say why she cried then but now I knew. I tried to imagine him, this dead brother, as he runs and runs toward the German tank but I never see the end, he just keeps running, and only Germans are dead. This happened near the town of Olovo where the future president of the UN and later of Austria was photographed with his troops.

Her guilt was huge, a word I learned looking at her. If only she hadn't left him in order to escape that horrible man, he wouldn't be dead now. She would be dead, what bad luck she had to stay alive, she moaned. I kept thinking, wait a minute, had you died and not escaped that horrible man, why would your son necessarily be alive? Isn't it better that someone lived to tell the story? And what about Stojan and me? Did she forget we had to be born. Her guilt was so huge she couldn't stand it, she had to push it away by imagining some other outcome, someone else to blame. And the only person to accuse presently was — who else but Dad because this child would have survived if he had been with us during the war. Why wasn't he? I ask.

"He didn't want him with us," she says.

"Dad? I thought you said he loved kids so much."

"He did after you were born, not before. Then it was too late. The war broke out, he couldn't come," she says. Which means that it was the war's and the Germans' fault, not Dad's, I come to his aid silently.

"You mean he said, tell him to come, and he couldn't do it?" I ask.

"Yes," she says.

"Why? Because there were no trains?"

"No trains, no roads, nothing."

"So," I conclude openly this time, "if he had said yes, it's not his fault, is it?" If you are going to blame people, at least blame them for what they did, right?

She didn't like my questions or my attempt to know the whole truth. She preferred her explosions, that's how she got her satisfaction. What's more, she could unite all her grievances in one. My constant need to know came from her own need to cover up; bit by bit, I decided she was wrong to blame him for this. One, she left the baby, this now-dead brother, even before she had met Father, and she wouldn't have invited him to live with us even if the war hadn't broken out, because this first marriage was a secret kept from everyone, even her best friends. It had to do with some silly idea about divorced women. Shame and such. All those wrong, stupid bourgeois notions that socialism tried to destroy along with veils, dowries, nationalism, and superstition. For all her strength and bravado, Mother was a very traditional woman with small-town views about good name, reputation. She herself would not be too happy if, let's say, Stojan decided to marry a divorced woman with a child, although that would be better than not marrying at all. No, I decided, he was not to blame. Not for this. Not guilty. She later said I should have been a lawyer or a judge, that's how she saw me.

She regretted this moment in the kitchen right away. It made her more vulnerable to other questions, our need to know more which she never satisfied because she preferred a more mythical, shadowless past, or because she didn't want to touch her pain. It made it worse, she said, refusing each time. It's best to keep it sealed. You can't understand that, you are only a child, she said, forgetting that kids have their own miseries. In my view still, they are bigger than anything grownups have for all sorts of obvious reasons.

Why had she been forced to get married, I kept thinking, why was this man so awful, what did he do exactly, what could it be, it had to be unspeakably bad to force her to run away or she would have died. She said she tried to kill herself twice. When you don't know, you imagine worse. How did she try to kill herself, for example, — with a gun or a knife? A river? Which river was it? Did she jump and they saved her? How else can you kill yourself? No matter how hard I tried, she never told any more, that day or later. Maybe she wanted to keep it to herself, that pain that was so big you can't tell others about it or you diminish it, the way I now can't tell, or I refuse to chat about recent trips to Yugoslavia even though they urge me to, tell us about it, how was it, do tell, and I think what would they understand if they don't know all the details, the way we were once. My refusal angers people, it's stingy, why can't you share, and the truth is it would add zest to a cocktail hour on the Upper West Side.

Maybe she was afraid that the pain would take hold of her, become as real as it was then. It must have been unbearable because she didn't mind talking about the Germans and the bombs. She tried to kill this one as best as she could while I searched and probed in order to know her better. Maybe it's the part we hide that matters more, maybe it's a clue of sorts. Each time I thought about those summers in Chicago, my head turned and I would stop, afraid of some horror I couldn't name. However, I couldn't erase it, alter it: I knew it was there. My mother had a talent for covering up the bad, a gift for becoming someone else through laughter, jokes, escaping, insisting on the good times, no matter how. But in order to create the imaginary life, she needed help and allies. She wanted me to hate him with her and that I couldn't do. I didn't hate him.

I looked at him instead, this frail, short man I was supposed to resemble. Sometimes, when I succeeded, I found my dad, the one who had carried me in the snow, laughing, but that hadn't happened often. For the most part, he was this other guy, a lost person — the same word that he used to describe immigrants around us. Former men, he said, for variety. That's what we are.

Men who have lost everything become lost in their turn for obvious reasons. They have nobody to remind them daily who they were and that they have lost their familiar rivers, towns, and hills, too. Lost became a permanent word in my thoughts along with "I remember," and "the way we used to be." We were similar after all, Dad and me. He said "lost" all the time. He didn't have a gift for make-believe, called it lying or pretending, nor did he have the ability to change anything. As a result, his honesty about others and himself was total and deadly. It made you wonder if honesty is a better way out or if it has nowhere to go; at least Mother enjoyed herself while pretending. I couldn't make up my mind, which is better — since a part of me aimed for truth while the other portion wished to escape, so sometimes I felt bad for him, other times for her, but less so. I couldn't imagine what it felt like to be her, a woman who is told she is old with wrinkles. I had no wrinkles and she was not the person you felt sorry for. In spite of the deep wrinkles on her forehead, she was attractive, bursting with life, you just couldn't think "There goes a lost woman, a former person." And she had something extra, her treasures, her gold, all her worldly possessions — what she called us. Her gifts to him. His bad luck not to appreciate us or her, she said.

She definitely had us, and I suppose we had her.

Chapter Eight

They fought openly now, even in the morning. Sunday lunch was the worst, all four of us at the table. Slowly, the hostilities would spread to include Stojan and me; we couldn't escape their war. Anything could provoke it, the smallest, seemingly innocent gesture, like "pass me the salt' from him to Stojan who was either absent-minded or unused to orders without sweet words — would send him into a fury because "pass me the salt" meant right away, this minute. Then a dish broken, and he would rave, "Nobody listens to me, nobody respects me, I'm nothing but a horse's ass."

With dishes breaking, and his shouts, the dog next door would bark. Then the old man would add his own shouts at the dog. In Lithuanian, I think. Our Sunday music with lunch.

Why couldn't Stojan pass him the damn salt shaker right away if it caused so much trouble? The first few times it looked like he was absent-minded and no more, but then, later, it was obvious that there was more to it. Stojan was saying no, under the cover of silence and fruit pies; he was waging a passive resistance of his own. He was not used to men, or to taking orders from them. Mother punished him, but she hugged too; he knew he was loved at all times. "My little man," she called him. He was at the center of her heart. Father did nothing of the sort; he even disliked her endearments, strangely jealous, it appeared, that none were for him. So he made fun of her and her unusual expressions when she called me "my son" and Stojan "my daughter." Of course there was no logic in this, but she liked it better; in her mind, this reversal made for bigger endearments, and it was original. Other people didn't do this, just her. If only she had called him something sweet or personal, everything would have been fine, I kept thinking. Maybe.

Suspended in the void, I took no sides. He was the father I had longed for, he was my memory of that word love. I knew he had loved me once. He didn't have to tell me; we knew it. She, who had not cared for me in that special way reserved for Stojan — my sugar, my sweet, my little man — now expected me to be without doubt or reserve on her side. She knew I had loved him as a child and, because of this, she couldn't trust me one hundred percent, be sure which way I would go in matters of allegiance. It bothered her. She had to win me over.

"You can't touch them," she told him which meant he couldn't beat us, either with a stick or his hand. Only she could. He almost slapped Stojan after the first salt shaker episode, but she was faster. "I will pluck your eyes out," she told him, "if you touch them." We were hers, she said, because she gave birth to us and only a mother knows how to hit hard enough but not too hard. He can't have these privileges because he did nothing all those years except save his own ass in a foreign country and then to fool around with an ugly German slut. Fool around registered without knowing how you do it. Slut I knew because we had several sluts in my neighborhood, women who got beat up at night and then my grandma healed them with her herbs in the morning. Sluts were friendlier and more generous in my kid experience than women who were not sluts and yet they often had bruised cheeks and arms. On the other side, fooling around seemed like playing, a nice thing to do. It didn't go well with that word slut. That word slut —I like the way it sounds in English, is only a translation. Our word is not the same and has a different meaning, it's not bad and they, the sluts, didn't think they were bad either. Nobody used the word 'bad' at home, like "bad girls"; we had and often used a word for shame but not guilty, guilt. It takes two words to say guilty. So, while I didn't know the real meaning of the word 'guilty' until the day Mother told her story in the kitchen everyone including me and the sluts knew the word 'tragic'. Like my tragic life, and my tragic destiny.

In a short time, my parents went far and did what only "bad" families do — unacceptable behavior — they fought in front of others whenever they could. It escalated beyond that slut to include their national differences that I had been unaware of. He said how in Montenegro people don't have an ear for music, their songs are nothing but one-tone laments; she knifed him with her reply that yes, they might not know how to croon and use face creams but they know how to fight and grow tall, handsome, each one six feet; the shorter and less handsome ones are left to die at birth. Was this true or invented? I knew, or at least she said they sometimes abandoned female children at birth. Then came all those old stories about men who courted her, each begging, each handsomer and richer and what does she do but marry a sickly short man who soon after disappears instead of taking care of us. And she, who at home was so proud that he left with the king's army, had different words for it now.

Once again the ground shifted under my feet. I couldn't believe it. It was never done, our family secrets openly told, even when she punished us nobody ever knew. Now she could hardly wait for a chance to tell some peasant about everything; she complained to whoever would listen. Something was shattered for good in East Chicago. Without our town to define us, to set the rules, what, who to be, how to behave, keeping up the façade no longer mattered. Or else she was so angry, so out of control, she didn't even notice all this and only said what popped into her mind. They both did that.

Yet in all this, she never fell apart; she never forgot to cook, wash, or eat. Her appetite was fine. Like a clever military leader, a head of state, she was perhaps only consolidating her position, making sure whom to have on her side. Once again she had us in the kitchen around the table, in the same deadly heat with him away, and said, low, with an air of finality, "Yes, I can't deny it, it's all been a mistake. We shouldn't have come." There it was, in her own words. A part of me wished she hadn't said it, I could then doubt my own thoughts which she had now confirmed. I also wished she had some plan to make things better, but she didn't. "What's done is done," she said, "it's too late, we can't go back, where to?" Everything we had was sold or given away —, our beds, our table, our sheets— another family already sleeps in our old place. That was too hard, it stopped your imagination of return. I couldn't imagine other kids jumping through my window, playing in our garden!

That was final. We had nothing now. In spite of all this, I said, "Let's go back anyway.

We don't need much. So what if we don't have sheets."

However, even if everything had remained the same, she couldn't go back now because it would be too humiliating. It was out of the question. Her enemies would rejoice to see her looking like a sick beast. She could never give them that pleasure, oh no. What enemies? I didn't know she had that many. Mother had a slew of them, it turned out, real and imaginary, all waiting for revenge, to laugh at her pain, her failure, and that triumphal exit, as she and her kids decked out in their best clothes left for the promised land where only bliss awaited them. We had been the first to leave. Not many left after we did because they didn't have anywhere to go, nor did they like leaving their living relatives or the dead.

She should have stopped here. She should have guessed that I too had lost my dreams, funny how that word "lost" kept coming up all the time, sad how at fifteen I was looking back instead of looking at the present. She didn't spare me, because she wanted to get everything off her chest. It was not premeditated; she only wanted to feel better. This new revelation was reserved for me alone so maybe it was planned after all because she would have been too ashamed to talk like that in front of Stojan. My first woman-to-woman talk. "He is dirty," she said, "he smells bad, he doesn't wash, and I shouldn't say all this because you're only a child." This didn't stop her from talking. It was vague. Was she getting brainwashed from those commercials? Was she trying to tell me he was too dirty to have in the same bed? "You are only a child, I really shouldn't," she repeated. You could tell him to wash, I wanted to say, you could get him to use Prell or Ivory, he could gargle with Listerine; sad how he became "him," even for me. At home he was always Daddy, Dad in my thoughts.

"I didn't notice he smelled bad," I said, which was true. He didn't. She looked at me and sighed, "Ah, what do you know, you are just a kid." I knew she was definitely covering up. I didn't know what it was. It had nothing to do with bathing, that much I knew.

In spite of the hostilities, or because of them, we tried a new activity one Sunday afternoon. At home this was called visiting, a moderately boring time when we went to see all sorts of grownups who talked to each other about historical events, marriages and births. It lasted forever. They whispered, a hand over a mouth, eyebrows raised about mysteries on our street, (Don't say! After only five months! They say the baby looks like you know who) while we ate fruit pies or cakes with schlag and looked at their family albums when they were handsome and young. (Ah, they said, eh, what's a life, it's over before you blink). You learned many things on these visits — patience, how to behave, how not to yawn, how to pretend to be deaf, how to get absorbed for hours in some photo until the picture grew alive. Afterwards, the three of us went to the park, and sometimes we sat in a cafe by the waterfall, a cool place even in summer.

Now, just like at home, we got dressed up first: Mother powdered her face, I wore my white dress and wedgies with no socks, father one of his blue English suits, Stojan had his long pants on. Dressed this way, feeling festive and important, we were going to promenade for a while, a very pleasant activity you did every evening after dinner on the main street. It was the most exciting time of day, everyone was there, young and old, and you noticed the new dress, or the new haircut and the new boy. We took up most of the sidewalk along Chicago Boulevard, and we walked this way with no competition, surprised somehow not to see any people. Obviously, it was too early in the day, you only promenade at night. We continued; a sidewalk changed into a path and we had to go single file, the dust thick under our feet. On our left, bushes and bits of garbage, cans, papers; on the right, cars. Drivers appeared annoyed at us for some reason, they said things we didn't understand and sometimes they threw things through the window — a Coke bottle, paper plates. My wedgies were no longer white. Mother's powder was gone. It didn't occur to us that we looked funny, that nobody walked along the highway in America. Father should have told us. We walked and walked for a long time. Then, on the other side of the railroad tracks, suddenly we saw a family coming toward us. They were well-dressed as if for a wedding, and we knew they were ours without bothering to ask them. They looked the way we must have looked too — hopelessly lost on the edge of the highway, miserable, sweaty. Old habits die hard. Ages later, when I was walking along the highway from Silver Lake to West Hollywood, cops stopped me. "What are you doing?" they said, and I said with some anger, "Isn't it obvious?" then remembered us that first summer. Our sad attempt to live, to be normal.

Our walk had an aim — to visit five peasants who lived together in a section which had people of different colors on the street. I preferred this neighborhood to ours, where you saw nobody ever except in cars. There was music, laughter, the smell of cooking, and, on the sidewalk, two girls played hopscotch. I couldn't believe it. It was amazing. They played just like us! They played jump rope too. I wanted to linger. I was good at hopscotch. Even at a distance, they looked wonderful, all movement, everything flying — arms, legs, cotton dresses.

The house with our men was something else; it looked abandoned inside and outside, gray, peeling wall paper. The men were surprised, happy we had come, ashamed they hadn't cleaned up. If only they had been warned. There was no way; they had no phone. Squalor of this sort was new to me. It was interesting once you got used to it — unwashed dishes, garbage overflowing, the smell of dirty socks. Flies and big roaches on the floor. These guys were super-dirty, the dirtiest ever — but with Lysol it would all go away, didn't they know? They shook their heads, grinned like kids, a house without a woman is cursed, one of them said. Mother looked at Dad and us, her head high. "You should be grateful," her eyes said. "Former men,"

Dad muttered, as always including himself in that pile.

The former men ate chunks of meat and offered us some. Beer, a repulsive taste, bitter. They questioned us in detail about things at home; they had heard on the radio how thousands were in prison and you could never go to church. I urged them to go back, hoping to persuade her too. If we returned, I was sure everybody, including Dad would immediately become who they once were. I don't remember how we got back; it had to be the same old way.

Mother said the following day that these men lived like animals, they even had a black woman who came to see them once a week. Imagine, she said, just imagine the same one for all five. I couldn't imagine anything. So what, I kept thinking, if a woman visits them, we visited them too. Then she said that Dad had lived in the same house with those men for a while, and most likely he saw the same woman too. She didn't expect me to understand; she was talking to herself for the most part. Later, I thought about this woman and a new obsession took hold of me — maybe I had a brother or a sister who was half-black and one of those days we would meet. How wonderful that would be, I trembled imagining it — a different scenario each time — but the very best one was when we recognized each other without any words. This consoled me about that other brother I had lost, and they both looked the same — tall, very handsome, and dark. Was this an attempt to make America my own? Whatever it was, it took hold and didn't change over the years. Again and again, in Paris, or at home in Yugoslavia, I would miss a certain black America in music, laughter, or the rhythm of words. It wasn't intellectual or political; it was just one of those things. I am jumping ahead but what can you do, our thoughts don't move in a straight line.

So there we were. Our promenading stopped. Mrs. Jones and Mr. Smith continued to act on the tape recorder in the heat. They never became friends or did anything interesting, just gab gab about the weather and their lawns. What lawns? No matter how bad it was in Chicago, Mother had set her mind on staying. She said we'd better get used to it; the other part was over. It was easier for her because she had tons of energy, of hope forever renewed, which permitted her to find joys no matter how small or temporary. She could laugh over and over again about some silly phrase some peasant had used; she imitated his gestures, his walk, then added bits and pieces of her own to the original score. It occurred to me later that her approach to life was artistic, without art. Or living was her art form, and she could pour it all out unsparingly on her first draft, knowing there was always more, and she could rewrite everything anytime she wanted to. She even got pleasure out of winning fights with Dad. The rest of us were less gifted. Stojan grew pudgy and soft; I retreated to a planet of my own without anyone noticing.

In the midst of all this, Dad tried to win big by gambling on football scores in England. He had gotten used to it over there and twice had won large sums, betting on the same team. That was before we came. He said we had done something to his luck. He had never lost before: either he had broken even or he had won. It had to be our fault, since we were the only new element in his life. He didn't give up, however, and tried a new approach — he asked me to tell him the name of the winning team. He hoped his luck would change, not that it ever did.

He said that the crazy man with red hair was absolutely right when he told him not to bring us over; he had been better off before. If only we could reverse his luck, if only he could win, I kept thinking. If only I could do magic, I kept wishing, although I knew it was hopeless —even if he won, so what! There was nothing either he or I wished to buy with that money or, if we did, it wouldn't have changed much. Nothing of importance; money is not the childhood wish.

Chapter Nine

Everything was stacked against him from the beginning; poor Father didn't even know how to tell his own story. He was more timid, less inventive or gifted, with less urge than she had, and he didn't know how to push and shove to get his view across. I should have pushed him to tell more, but there was no mystery in him that I was dying to know, no special secrets about his life. His tale was all of a piece, always the same, always woes and loneliness rather than an attempt, no matter how small, to make himself into a hero, to give himself a major role. He was never the center of attention even in his own stories, even for him, even in his imagination; that was the problem. That's why he couldn't tell his story well. The few times he tried without any of the flamboyance or exaggeration we were accustomed to from you know who, his words appeared pale, uninteresting to listen to, he lacked the habit of her oral tradition perfected over the centuries — you repeat the story of your life over and over again, repeat it until others absorb it without being aware of it. That's how it was for five centuries under the Ottomans, and each generation absorbed the tales of our glorious past, our kings, our art, everything we were before the Turks enslaved us. Mother just continued in the same epic style which he, educated, forgot or moved away from. To me, this proved that peasants are stronger.

Here is the saddest part: his own stories — that is, those meant to be just his, those that happened only to him — were much better told by her, and, what's more, later we remembered them as hers — how they had met in this beautiful city on the Adriatic coast, and how he had fallen in love with my mother one day. It was so unbearably romantic and a bit sad because he was sick in the hospital with the bone illness that would plague him his whole life when in a moment of rest, between two injections, he saw this young healthy woman with a basket of fruit in her arms. Then she would say, "Life is strange. I never thought I would marry this puny sickly man." Why did you? we wanted to say, not daring. And of course we knew what she admired — tall dark ones who were, I suspect, on the mean side — her contradiction — no wonder she always said she had never met a man who was right for her. Never, never once. How could she? I ask you.

It never occurred to her that she could hurt with words like sickly, puny, short, yet she herself was stung right away at the mildest unflattering remark. So his important story about their first meeting always became hers. In it, she was both a man looking at her, the woman he saw, and a woman being looked at. Her final conclusion was simple, "You only have healthy good-looking children because of me." It was amazing how she did it, and nobody said, "Hey, wait a minute!" not even him. Or another sad story about how he became an orphan because his poor mother died at birth leaving him loveless forever, and his horrible stepmother beat him while his father drank, all potentially perfect tragic events that explained him and his shyness, why he was never at the center of anybody's heart even in his imagination, a story so sad it should have made us cry. She would interrupt and say, "Yes, that's how it is, once you lose your mother you lose everything. Fathers don't give a shit, and you better not lose me, because you wouldn't have survived had you been left with him instead of me." "Men just chase whores," she would add for a finale, unforgiving forever, subverting his story for her own gain. Then they would bark at each other, in a fight he was bound to lose.

Thinking about this, a part of me cringes, not fair and such, and yet another portion is all admiration before this pure brute force you find in forests or jungles, and is the reason why only the fastest sperm gets to the goal. In their arguments, which had a function as entertainment or self-expression, there was no attempt to be fair or logical (my obsession with fairness was an old one), she didn't say that she hated her mother (but I knew she did) who never did anything good for her, and that she, too, liked her dad very much, and she forgot that my dad began sending packages from England as soon as he was able to. He even came to the U.S. because that's where she wanted to go, not England, not her, why would she bother with a country with gray skies, cold, unkind to strangers. Thank God my memory is good, I keep everything as evidence in order to compare, you could go crazy listening to her, she could invent whatever she wanted on the spur of the moment and make your head spin wondering. I mean she could even invent my own life — even the parts only I know. She had done it before. I had to keep everything, a precaution against madness, I remember even silly details without importance, useless undramatic pieces she would have thrown away. You just never know, I might need them some day. I have been trained to remember, all alone, mind you, to make sure it's me all the time. Nobody could rewrite me, nobody. My head is full of facts, when who said what. It's too bad to have to remember constantly, all the time, it stops you, all that excess of memory prevents your moving forward. You are heavier this way, maybe the right word for it is older. She didn't worry about trivia or accuracy, free to invent her life, alter, add, or destroy an unpleasant past, and yet she never worried that she would go mad, splinter. I could never imagine what it must be like inside her soul, what thoughts she had upon waking up.

In Mother's fits of anger, she forgot we lived from those packages Father had sent, all those nylon blouses, raincoats, stockings others were jealous of. How she loved it all. She didn't work after that — the packages began to come regularly every month. All that was forgotten because he had showed her a picture of some dumb German slut. Get a grip on yourself, I wanted to say, be fair. The woman wasn't even nice to look at.

I didn't reproach him for this woman; she was just a photo and no more. He was lonely there, I reasoned, she made him less so. If she did that, that was fine. It sounds like she was not stingy. Didn't Mother always say that the worst sin is to be stingy? He had nobody in that cold town in Germany. Mother had her neighborhood, her sister, her aunt and us. She had us even at night, next to her in the twin beds moved together so we could sleep one on each side. Most important of all, she had her language. If you lose that, who are you? No, I didn't reproach him for the same things as I reproached her. If I reproached him for anything, it was his stupidity; why did he have to show her that damn picture, what was going on in his dumb head? I don't think it was intentionally cruel. He had simply lived too long among men, had forgotten how women think, and he was stupid enough in some book tradition to believe that if they were both honest about everything, their past etc., they could start all over again. It smells of the movies to me. He had expected her to have known other men, wouldn't have been hurt, she said, but you never know what would have happened if she had said yes.

You never know anything with my family, but I do know one thing — she would never have said yes, not her. For one, she would have had no need to tell, confess, and her thoughts were more military, bigger in the epic mode, with tricky power struggles at all times. Mother wouldn't have shown him any dumb picture or told him anything that later could be used against her. He lacked her peasant cunning, his faults were Prince Mishkin's, I thought. I had made a mistake. The Idiot was the last book I read. Not The Brothers Karamazov.

If you can't be sure of anything, you can only imagine, consider all possibilities. Maybe he wanted to show off, like, "Look, Mom, who I met!" to impress her a bit, make him seem more worthy. He never had a mother, poor guy, or anyone who could call him my treasure, my sweet, my gold. Still, let's say he never did it, nothing, no picture, no words, let's say that ugly Helga didn't exist, it would have still been too late for him and her. Too many years in between, too, too many. It was too late that first day at the train station because they didn't know how to imagine each other's lives. He couldn't see our house bombed, me injured, her all alone left to feed us, for him we remained in the world he had loved, he wanted to keep it intact. For him our large sunny white kitchen had not been destroyed by the bomb, in it he remained that officer with the saber and both of them are forever young. In that other kitchen, his kids are always running toward him for a hug, his friends cheer, toast, there are parties, masked balls. Then the Germans arrived.

The Germans are not in my memory as long as he is with us. If he had stayed, I used to think as a child, the Germans would not have arrived. I retain the last day, the last moment in front of the house, the one Stojan doesn't remember, the one which will be destroyed in a month. Mother holds him in her arms. I am by her side. In front of us, on the street, all sorts of soldiers pass, heavy coats, heavy boots, horses, mud. Dad hugs me and hugs until it hurts. He is crying, be good to them, don't punish them too much, he says. Then, soon, right away, like on the next page, the planes appear, and the men in gray helmet, and everything falls apart. Our all-white kitchen, my organdy dresses, my toys.

If anyone should be blamed for our misery then and now, I reasoned, it should be Hitler, who else, can't they see that, the evil came from the outside, it's not our fault, I kept thinking, my attempt at a larger picture. That's why later I couldn't take the American dream seriously, all that part about how you try and try and then you can become anything you wish, even the President.

Baloney, I say, then and now. No amount of trying and working hard would have kept our house intact, would it? The same with other houses near us, and all those people who died. Some generations are simply unlucky with history, but history is not something Americans like or understand too much. And for a reason. This kind of thinking is pessimistic they say, try hard cheer up, start all over. Sure, sure, but sometimes it's too late to start all over when all the springs are broken, and the inner parts have rusted, or have died. They don't understand this kind of thinking in the U.S., nor the tragic outcomes, or maybe they would if someday the planes came shrieking and their kitchens blew up. Then I would ask them about starting all over and cheerfulness. It sounds as if I were wishing for it. Yes, some days I do. Only in thought. I wouldn't really want it.

Starting all over — he couldn't do it. And she was no better at imagining what wasn't hers. She couldn't see his life away from us, as he retreated through the mountains, the country in flames, Germans and more Germans, and we also had the civil war. We are really gifted at civil wars in Yugoslavia, and it's no wonder that everyone is full of so many past gripes and they all want to rewrite each other's stories. And, in addition, the geography is bad; the country has too many neighbors, the sort of land you walk over. Dad's army went kaput. While the king saved his ass in England, Dad had to rot in Germany, one camp, another camp, England finally, where he is with men like himself, drifting, forgetting who they used to be. Lost. I am trying to tell the story he couldn't tell, the parts she couldn't imagine. Mother had no gift for hearing others, she listened and spoke to herself only. Like all those other egomaniacs, presidents, heads of state, military chiefs, just them and always them, me and me. Mind you, it doesn't mean that I was able to imagine his life either at that time, drifting, full of my own sadness, and my only excuse is that I was not a grownup. This objective truth does not make me feel better now. I blame myself in waves of regret that I was not able to imagine him the way I do now.

Much, much later, when I found him again, when we could have talked, it was too late. He was dead. We never had that conversation when I would listen to him and he would listen to me and he would know I cared. It is tragic to know the answer when it's too late. In his diaries he had recorded each day, what happened, what he thought, what he dreamt as he retreated. "Dreamt of Nadja," I read. "She is wearing a white dress. Is she ill or dead — isn't the white color the worst?" he asks, and worries constantly, page after page. Later, as he grew more lost, he worried less. The dreams are fewer in his entries, he asks fewer questions; he doesn't try to interpret them. His entries are shorter and shorter, a sentence here and there — then it all stops. So, on his own soil, retreating in the mountains of Bosnia, he wrote five pages for one single day, while in England the sole entry for 1950 is, "I guess I am going to America. I can't imagine Chicago." Nothing more after that. Nothing mattered so much after he left home.

I am not trying to say that he was without faults, but his good points meant nothing to her. All those grammar books Italian, German, and English, dictionaries, words carefully underlined, with question marks, a pile of index cards with new words to learn every day, to master this impossible language with illogical prepositions. "Imagine this," he would say. "They say 'Hurry up' to a person standing at the top of the stairs, while it should be hurry down, don't you think?" He argued with English, then searched for the meaning of a new word in the newspapers and grew frustrated when his dictionary didn't have it. He didn't know his dictionary was out of date, and, of course, I didn't know it either. He complained that American English is sloppy, that they don't speak correctly, the reason they don't understand him at times. He insisted I learn it correctly, say nobody, he said, it's not 'nobary', the way they pronounced it in Chicago. They changed the d's into r's for reasons that made no sense. "It is not *kent* but *kant*," he said, waving his arm, "I don't care if they say it." He regretted having left England where he had good luck with football teams, and they understood everything he said, and he preferred the way they dressed, and they knew how to foxtrot. He was never consoled that he spoke better than other immigrants around us because they didn't know their own language well, he said.

Books were not important to her, or books were just books. You can't eat them, smell them, nothing to look at. They were so different; that was the reason he fell in love, except he was not in love any longer. Now, their differences, who they were before the love, showed more clearly. Without all those missing parts, our country, our ways, they stood separated for me to look at, the way you examine characters in a play — him, a crazy intellectual I would meet in other places — her, a peasant with force and cunning, angry at anything abstract. Fuck your prepositions, she would say, you can't eat the verbs. She disliked the people who put on airs, or pretended they were better in those areas she didn't understand. Books were not real life, that's all there was to it, books were many steps removed from real life in which she was involved full blast. She appreciated men who knew how to fix things, repair faucets, make shelves, men who knew how to build a house, make wine, or cut a perfect leg of lamb. In the same way, later, she viewed my college degrees as something useful, almost tangible, you hang them on the wall in a nice frame. Dad wanted to know just to know, for no reason, it led nowhere, it couldn't be cashed in, it had no ambition attached. She was better suited to Chicago, no doubt about it. His view on race, for example was very original for that time. When I asked him, the only time we ever spoke about this subject, how come you never see black and white people together or couples of different races, he said, "Why not, indeed? As far as I am concerned, both black and white cows give the same kind of milk."

I am not saying it was easy for her — my father was not like her nor was he like other people. Take flies for example, hundreds of them in the summer months, all over the food. As she chased and killed, he would let them land on his hand or fork and as she created killing fields on the floor, he would look up and then say, "How would you feel, I ask you, if someone stepped on you?" I suspected him of feeding the roaches.

He tried making contact with me, he believed I had not changed. He spoke about verbs and prepositions; later, when I knew more than he did, he begged me to tell him the meaning of this or that word in the women's magazines full of ads for face creams. If you use Ponds, he said, all the wrinkles disappear. I don't know why he didn't reject this, the way he did many harder things, why he didn't say, what rubbish, what stupidity. Maybe because it was so ordinary he didn't notice it, maybe he liked pretty girls, or, I suspect, he identified with their weakness. At that time, in the fifties, men had it easy — they didn't have to be handsome or fit —nobody looked at them anyway, not 'that way,' nobody except gay men, but that's a whole other story. There wasn't much a man had to worry about, judging from the ads — sure, there were pimples, bad breath, and dandruff, but girls had this and more. Men had to look powerful, though — that was the main thing — either with height or bulk or money, and my father had none of those things. I think he wanted to look good for someone, someone to please, most people do. He had a clear idea of beauty, however, just his; he sneered at the stars on the screen, "Her, pretty?" he would say. "I wouldn't have her as a maid." His sneering was always directed at the screen, a picture of the same star in Mademoiselle or Glamour didn't provoke him — maybe because it was less realistic, it didn't move; it was fixed. Men were excluded entirely from all this, either in beauty or admiration. I don't remember a single man he admired. He loved soft, fragile, gentle; he loved kids. He told me that Englishwomen have a fine skin like porcelain due to humid air and absence of sun, and of course they take care of themselves. This was a new idea for me. The notion of 'taking care of yourself' didn't exist, nobody bothered beyond the usual. "What's the point?" they would have asked. He talked as if he knew everything about this subject, and, what's more, he looked very young for his age, no doubt about it. Did he use those beauty creams in secret? He also had a full head of hair, no wrinkles anywhere. Was it because he grimaced in front of the mirror so much or because he didn't suffer, as Mother claimed. She also said blond people always look younger because they remain chicks forever. A peasant expression for those less powerful, less dark, and in this I was included.

Chapter Ten

Mother carried a huge bag of imaginary optimism; even her rage proved she was still herself. It was not the same for the rest of us, each lost separately. She had a function, things to do, cook and clean, make more lace, and then she was seized with a new project all of a sudden — she'd prove to everyone back home how happy we were. We had pictures taken, first an official one in a studio, for which we got dressed up. We traveled by bus to Indiana Harbor known as the 'Mexican town.' I wore a white blouse you could pull off the shoulders for a Spanish style, or it could go up for a more subdued look, a photographer insisted on lipstick, blouse off the shoulder and a smile; you don't notice right away my eyes look borrowed, not mine. All of us look dreadful in that picture, but Mother didn't see it that way. She knew that this group picture sent to my aunt would be seen by everyone in the way it was intended. They'd marvel at us. They did, even though we looked dead and dug up, me all bones, Stojan so grim,

Dad mean-looking, like Oswald if he had lived longer. Soon, she'd discover that you didn't have to go an expensive studio for pictures; in America everybody had a camera, you could photograph yourself all the time. We did, with other people's cameras. In front of a cannon in some park, in front of that sickly tree so it looked like we had others, in front of, on top of cars, Buicks, Cadillacs, so it looked like we owned them. However, I became the prime target of those pictures because men liked photographing me, leaning against this or that, head thrown back, in contorted poses borrowed from some star. It was easy. It was in those women's magazines Dad had around the house. It filled the void, and the photos had a reality of their own. The girl in the pictures was wonderful-looking, and she could change all the time. She wasn't me, I didn't think of her as me. She was a girl in between. I existed because of her, photos were my only proof.

Photos led me to a mirror, a major discovery. In the past, I had used it casually, in passing when combing my hair, but no more. Now, I stared into it for a long time, for hours, sometimes disappearing. She is gone. It's restful, you think why not try a new hairstyle, put it behind the ears, let's see what she'll be now. Lipstick, never permitted before but permitted now each time we took pictures, was a big help in transforming me into her. That summer my existence is in this — dresses, pictures, mirrors, that's all I have. I am in the surface of things, what you see or touch, the rest is gone, it feels like I took off in that imaginary plane and we had no place to land.

Through some unwritten rule, in our letters we perpetuated the lie, everything bad was omitted, the heat and our fights. In the photos we looked more and more prosperous and better dressed each month. Her part-time job as a cook enabled us eventually to buy more clothes, and she could send things home without bothering to ask Dad about it — bathing suits, nylon raincoats, coffee. She loved sending those packages. But the lie which we had started had to be kept up. The one avenue I had to tell someone about my misery was gone; it had to be done in the beginning or else. Nobody saw through those letters, written by me for the most part to her various friends and mine; nobody noticed anything, except my doctor. He said he could tell that something was missing, he said I was not telling the truth. He saw through it because he was so lonely himself and knew how to hide; he recognized it in others. Maybe because he loved me more than anyone, he could read between the lines. Still, it was funny he was the one to talk about the truth.

I had tried to tell her about him once. Soon afterwards. I am maybe twelve or a bit more when he too got undressed. That was the first time. I didn't even count all those other times when he kissed me all over examining me. That lasted for years. But this one time I was scared. His face looked funny. I had to tell someone, how else could I go back to him again. Who was there except her? She had all those women yakking in the kitchen about the usual subjects, men, marriages, and miseries when I ran in trembling. I wanted to tell her and yet protect him, I took her outside away from those women, I thought she could see I was shaking. No, she was not worried but annoyed, what will her guests think. She said to stop spreading lies about a perfectly good man who had saved my life more than once. Of course he had, but now he was undressing himself in front of me, all naked, the very first man for the first time. I never lied and wasn't lying this time, strange how her words hurt more than anything he did. Now, in Chicago, after so many confessions from her, my dead brother, the other husband, Dad's slut and the general mood in our kitchen, I mentioned him again even though I had decided never to do it again. I didn't need to accuse him, I only wished she would know me better, she would see how unhappy I was. Look at me, I guess I was trying to say, I am not the girl in those pictures. It was not planned. It wasn't about him really.

We were in the kitchen, just the two of us. Once again she was on her favorite subject — what pigs men are — when I opened my mouth to tell her about him once more. Just the bare essentials, undressing and such and how I ran. I thought the timing was good, she had introduced the subject of men.

"He couldn't have," she said looking somewhere over my shoulder. I said nothing after that. She was telling me I was lying again, it never happened. "He is a such a good man," she said, never looking at me once. She wasn't about to change her view of him, she would lose him forever if she accepted my truth because she would have to judge him accordingly. Unwilling to do it, she chose her memory of him over me. He was good to us, no doubt about it, he gave money, he rushed in when I was ill in the middle of the night, he found medicine when there wasn't any, he had saved me once, twice, many times. All that was true, but so was the other part, that he kissed my shoulders for years, secretly, not that it was always unpleasant. Maybe she couldn't imagine him doing it. Her heroes and villains were clearly separated: he was a hero, and that was that, just like her father and her brother, even though my aunt had other views about those two.

I didn't insist or fight that day. It wasn't urgent. I had no grudge against him any more. It was more like pity that he was so good and yet out of control. He didn't hurt me the way she did. And what's more, I believed, he loved me, no doubt about it, he did. She doesn't care about me, I thought that day, or she would be concerned. If Stojan had told her, she would be. It was over with, finished. What was meant to be my story or my confession evaporated, leaving me in a dream state — it wasn't real, it happened to some other person. She was pleased I didn't insist. I wished I had not mentioned him. I had betrayed him and myself and for nothing, an ugly feeling, some useless rage. She didn't see him either —we had our permanent places assigned.

With the years I've changed my opinion about her. She loved me as much as she could love a girl child, in her mountain village they put a black flag on the house when a girl is born.

Didn't her own mother push her to marry? Wasn't her own mother forced? All this I know now and pity that girl, her, but I also feel tender regret for the child that was me. I was not as tough as she was.

She would have survived even in the camps, no doubt about it, she would have found a way, maybe bribed the guards, slept with, strangled a few, she wouldn't just lie down and die stupidly, not her. She had so much more of pure raw life that kept her going, she must have had it from birth to survive all sorts of horrors, that first marriage and other things she kept secret. There were chunks of time, years we couldn't account for, that tempted our imagination, why both of us became writers, my brother and I, and why she remained the most fascinating person ever, the one you couldn't quite know or explain. She never tried to explain herself, it would have been foreign to her. She didn't have to, not with all that life in her.

She tempted everyone with food when they came to visit. All those lonely men loved everything she put in front of them, and she loved watching them eat as if they had been starved for years. Her stuffed cabbage, stuffed peppers, risotto, musaka, hot dishes that tasted better than steak. This food, the noise of men eating, the wine they drank, kept her alive, or were a proof she was herself. The continuity of cooking, the taste and smell. With a glass of wine, my mother grew animated, like a drunken peasant, she told jokes; red in the face, she snapped her fingers, sang epic songs and tales about her past beauty and numerous suitors, while Dad, all gloom, sat in the corner. She had a gift for manufacturing joy, no matter how temporary. Oblivious to most people and the gloom in the corner, she was the composer, the music, and her own audience too. She was amazing. She still is.

With more wine, men grew relaxed and wanted me to sit on their knees. "Look at her skin," they stammered, "just like a ripe peach." Their hands were rough, their eyes full of tears.

She didn't like their words, I observed again. I had noticed it the first time, the day of our arrival when all those men came. Not the way I had expected it (don't you paw my daughter, you brute), but some other kind of dislike, unreal, hard to figure out; it was all brand new. Mother is your best friend, she used to say at home, only mother can love and never be jealous. She didn't have a mother's face now, she was jealous of me without knowing it. And I, ignorant, with no experience of this kind of jealousy, refused to believe I saw it. She couldn't be, you had invented it, I kept thinking using her own words about my doctor. Yet her eyes on me were not kind, she blamed me for something I didn't know. It's not true, it's not my fault, I've done nothing, I kept talking just to me.

"My skin was better than hers and you should have seen my waist," she said this time, after I had managed to forget the first. A strange new pain appeared, then fear. Who is she? who am I? I wondered. I have nobody, what if there is no me?

Then a miracle happened. It could have been this or that, the candles in front of our patron saint, her food, or my skin that made him appear, a man we called our savior. We recognized him right away, even though we had never met, just the way he stood in front of that church was different from others — grinning widely, arms open; he was more interested in kids than in some silly political talk. "I don't bother with church too much," he said to my mother. "All that incense makes me sneeze." Turning to my dad, winking at us, he said, "What's the matter with you? What's this gloom! Stop torturing your family. Let the people live!" Of course everybody laughed, even my father, a proof this man was special. It wasn't just the words but everything else about him that made you feel good all over, you couldn't imagine him angry or mean — he had decided long ago to live and have a good time. We began calling him the savior in private even though his name was Pavle. Same as Paul, with his appearance, our life changed immediately. That very day, instead of a horrible hot bus, we flew in his blue car, which appeared as big as a ship. We were at home in nothing flat, a minute or so, and fortunately everything was ready, prepared in advance as if awaiting his arrival — a rizotto with lamb, hot peppers, cherry strudel, and when Mother lit a candle in front of Saint Nicholas, he said that was his saint too. It was all nice, simple, like having a real friend or a neighbor. He ate nonstop, pausing to laugh. He lived all alone in a hotel room, poor guy; he appreciated our kitchen, us, our food. Like a captured giant, overwhelmed with peppers, he fell asleep on our sofa and Mother put a white handkerchief over his face so the light and the flies would not bother him.. We were overjoyed — he'd sleep, then much later there'd be coffee and cakes, then dinner — the entire day would be good.

Our savior was tall, neither fat nor skinny, but not too thin around the waist, with a fine face and beautiful hands. He had a beautiful smile too, always there as if amused by us or his thoughts, the kind of smile you see on statues in Ancient Greece. Only, if you paid attention, you saw that his eyes were not laughing. They were dark and very sad, the same eyes my doctor had. He had been an officer, like Dad; he had been raised by his aunt. He said he was an orphan from birth. Both parents died in the first World War. Before I met him, I had never thought of orphans as grownups.

He woke up soon, Mother served him coffee, we talked. The last bit of strudel gone, he said, "Now, soldiers, what do you say we go to the beach? You probably don't have any bathing suits, do you?" Was he kidding! We had everything ready, just for this day, the miracle of his appearance. Soon we headed past East Chicago, past the factories of Gary, all smoke on both sides, then smaller towns appeared with trees, and finally we saw only water and sand. Lake Michigan was pale green.

Unaccustomed to the heat, the lake like a reflecting mirror, we turned red fast but Stojan was himself again, laughing, diving, just the way he used to be. God, how happy he looked, how happy I was to see him that way. We didn't pay attention to other people on the beach that day, we didn't notice what we would later, that even babies wore bathing suits here. Then Pavle took us to a place where you eat in your car, we tasted hamburgers and ice cream in a large dish. He took many pictures of us that day at the beach. Mother said the next time he takes better pictures of me, since everybody else looked the way they usually do. I didn't recognize me as the girl in the picture. She was a girl in a pale blue bathing suit.

He came often, on Sundays. "Shall we swim or not?" he would say. Father didn't go after the first time, he said the sun made his head spin. He said it was boring at the beach. Coming back, sunburnt but feeling good, we found him in the same spot, in front of a dictionary, learning a new word, or sending a letter to England hoping his luck would change.

Later in my life, I imagined our savior's life in his dingy hotel room as he wondered whether he should come to visit us or not. Had we had an extra room, had we said come live with us, he would have said yes, I am sure. As it was, he would decide not to come every Sunday, he was a well brought-up man, an officer of the old school, it was not polite, he would think, to eat lunch with a family every week. From our side, we waited impatiently for him to appear. We grew fidgety. We missed him or we missed the beach as much. Then Mother would say, "Go call him, tell the old goat to hurry up!"

"Why me every time?" I said once.

"He won't say no to you," she said, matter-of-fact. I went to that corner bar, past the drunken men looking and the owner looking at me when I asked if I could use the phone. I didn't know which was worse the bar, or her words. He won't say no to you. It meant something I didn't know. He won't say no to you, I kept thinking, bothered that I didn't have a right word for that pain.

Chapter Eleven

Somehow the horrible summer ended and the fall began — not that you noticed the change by the smell of leaves or air. It just grew colder, that's all. I've lost one whole summer, now I'll lose an autumn, then winter too, I kept thinking. I used that word 'lost' for all sorts of things that year, but most often it meant life unlived, the one that couldn't be replaced. Then I lost Stojan to a school for lower grades. This was unexpected. I will have to go to mine all alone now, the same brick building with that tape recorder. With him around I feared less, calmed by his mood of indifference to most things. I'd not seen that expression on kids or him before, but recently I saw it on refugees from the civil war with faces made of stone, eyes fixed— there was no point in getting excited, better save your energy; it can get worse.

All alone, I worried that first day. For this occasion I wore my Sunday clothes, a white blouse and a white ballerina skirt with little blue flowers, white wedgies, pearls and earrings to match. Very long pageboy, hair lifted off my face with two clips. Dad said I looked better than any girl he had ever seen; he picked my clothes that day. I didn't notice right away that I looked different from others in school. They must have.

That day is fuzzy, like images from a moving train. I am so lost and nothing is real, not even the fear which twists my stomach in waves. It goes away by itself when I think, when I say, don't be afraid now, you are not here, it's not real, soon you'll wake up. The dream goes on and on, I can't wake up. In the halls, shiny and green, there are green lockers; one of them is mine, I'm told, or I'm guessing they tell me that. Why do I need it, what for? Why should I put my books in it, what books? Why are they running off to different classrooms? We had just one at home, and teachers came to us in a very orderly fashion. I had one and the same desk for the entire year. In Roosevelt High, with hundreds of students running from class to class, only two minutes in between, bumping into each other, yelling, banging those iron lockers, the mood of chaos dominated, fatigued you, and inside the class it was strange too. Teachers yelled, students whispered, blew gum, someone was constantly being led to the principal's office, but I didn't notice all that the first day. That day, I was mostly trying to figure out where I was, how to get to all those different rooms, what if I walked into a wrong class and they said something and I didn't understand, what if I were late, what if I vomited, what if they laughed. I didn't know why I was in such-and-such a class — somebody must have decided it. Why biology if I had already had it? Why beginners' chemistry when I should be doing biochemistry now or advanced physics, world history, advanced composition, French and Greek. I didn't understand either why students in the same grade had very different courses; it added to the confusion in the halls.

Nobody explained, and of course it would have been pointless, since I didn't speak English. I understood nothing the biology teacher said. He spoke faster and less clearly than Mrs. Jones and Mr. Smith. However, in the book I recognized words like osmosis, and pictures of cells dividing. Latin helped like an old friend in chemistry too. I'd had all this two years ago.

In English class they didn't read books or write compositions. Instead, they did something called diagramming which looked like a tree with verbs and nouns. Then there was something called civics, a speech class with a thin man called Ford, and gym where you had to wear very ugly puffed shorts. The strangest of all was the first class with no books and whose purpose was not clear to me. It was called home room, for some reason. A woman who looked like a plucked chicken called our names and couldn't pronounce mine. I corrected her, she tried. Then I gave up. Let her call me what she will, I decided. The class was getting too excited by her attempts, and by my name. The best part about that class and that day was the girl who sat next to me. She had chocolate skin, a very long neck, and the most beautiful, whitest teeth I had ever seen, and they were perfectly even. She pointed to my clothes, my face, and said 'pri'. By the way she smiled, I knew it wasn't anything awful, but I shrugged, not knowing what she had said. She wrote the word on a piece of paper which I took home. Then Dad lectured on how in the U.S. they don't know how to speak. It shouldn't be 'pri' but 'preti,' he said. Sloppiness, he insisted. Still, it was nice she called me that. When I hear "pretty" I think about her, a girl whose name I don't remember any more. I didn't know how to tell her she was beautiful, no doubt about it, she was, as beautiful, I thought that day, as the girls in Bali.

Stojan said nothing about his school, maybe there was nothing to say. He just turned the TV on again and drifted into his mood, call it indifference or bliss.

Days passed; September turned into October. I tried. Dictionary all the time. How I hate dictionaries still. You spend hours looking up every word and you still don't know what the sentence says. Some words can't be translated, some words were brand new. In both languages. Dad was overjoyed now, or at least he looked that way as he watched me suffer in front of that dictionary. Then I wrote all the new words in a little notebook he had bought for me. He asked, "How many, how many did you learn today?" It was all he wanted, new ones. "Don't worry," he said, "in six months you'll know more than they do. They just use the same five hundred words and never bother to learn more.

You will surpass them in six months." He was strange about words. They were like money to some people, maybe more than money, more than gold. Stojan kept up his silence, nothing about new words or about his school, not a single detail; he had decided to keep it to himself. It must be horrible, I thought, and didn't ask. It was better that way. He was free to tell me or not, and I knew he would have told me if things were not unspeakably bad. Dad didn't know him. Provoked by his silence, TV turned on full blast, he'd shout, he'd attack him, "You'll turn into a bum, you'll go work in the factory or worse, you'll be a beggar, a slave, go use the dictionary right now." This brought her cursing from the kitchen, "How dare you talk like that to your own flesh and blood. He is no bum, he is my son while you took your ass to..."

Even if Stojan had wanted to look up words, he couldn't have done it. Not in front of him. He had to resist him now, in order not give him any pleasure. We didn't know it then, being too caught up in our own misery, that Dad was really preaching at himself, he himself was a beggar, a bum, a slave. He didn't know it either. You can't know everything at fifteen, no matter how smart you are. Why is then my guilt toward him so huge if I was only a kid and he was supposed to be a grownup? But I was always a grownup at home, I worried about Mother and everyone. Why didn't I break the rules in Chicago to hug him in the morning? I knew him for a very short time — two years and three months.

I worried about Stojan, too; I couldn't get used to his new mood, which must have been a form of depression, a word we didn't know at that time. To shake him up, I dreamt up a new rescue plan one day — the one that would make everything better. It was meant to be like this — we would go out and then we would pretend to get lost. They would look for us. They would be so miserable, so worried, they would stop fighting, united in their love for us. They would weep, hug each other, swear to God never to fight again if only they could find us. The police would come, maybe with dogs. Dogs would sniff our clothes, and the search would start all over East Chicago. Which book did I steal this from? Stojan perked up, however; suddenly he was himself again, the same old Stojan who loved stories, who chased chickens and killed a few with a sling shot. Once again his eyes were alive.

We didn't elaborate on the plan. What if we really got lost? What if we were kidnapped by a witch in a car. What if our plane suddenly appeared? We were in too much of a hurry to worry about details, we didn't even take any food, the way you are supposed to.

So we set out to try to get lost, except it was better as a story. In real life, in East Chicago, it was too boring. No ravines, no mountains or creeks. Just more of the same symmetrical blocks and streets with numbers. We walked and walked; then it started to rain, and we had nowhere to hide. Drenched, we came back to 103rd Street. Nobody had even noticed that we had gotten lost. Can you imagine anything sadder than this?

I lost Stojan that year — or we lost each other — to other things. We would never again know or guess each other's thoughts; our troubles, worries, and joys would not be shared. I would stop worrying about him or trying to reach him; it was not intentional. We were overwhelmed. I grew silent too.

At school they said I was doing fine. Surprising, they said, A's and B's. That was good enough for them but not for me. I'd only had A's before, and, what's more, I was the best in my class, the one who always knew all the answers; my compositions were read all over the school, even by eighteen-year-olds. Never again. That was over. Here I just managed, nothing special. And I who had looked forward to every day at school dreaded it now. Fear and hidden humiliations lurked in the halls, and after school, too, when all the fat football players grunted at me all sorts of words I didn't know. Since I didn't understand anything the teacher said, I retained entire pages in my head, together with pictures, or I tried to guess what would be on the test. I examined the page carefully, reasoning that those topics which take up more space had to be more important; I memorized those entirely. It worked, but it was joyless, and I was not learning anything really. In English,

I did those boring diagrams, taught by Miss Swatz, who wore small bows in her hair and thick layers of lipstick coloring her teeth. She must have believed that diagrams would improve our minds or at least help us write correctly, but it didn't work that way since nobody understood what function they would serve in real life. You could get a passing grade for these things and yet never learn to write a single good sentence, the case with most kids around me. I felt bad for Miss Swatz because she had thin red hair through which her scalp could be seen. I felt sorry for her because each time the poor old woman tried anything different from those dangling participles — a sonnet for example, read beautifully with her eyes far away, half shut — the class laughed and laughed, especially the boys. She stopped reading then; her eyes hurt. She gave me an A for those diagrams, believe it or not — I was the best in her class, which was nothing to be proud of, not in that class. I couldn't understand why they couldn't do it, there was nothing to it once you learned the pattern. They didn't care that much about books or grades, mostly C's and D's, they only wanted a high school diploma and then a job in one of the factories around us. I guess they knew what was coming to them and those diagrams were just a waste of time, silly games never to be used. And I realized that here the diploma didn't mean much if anyone can get through.

Cars were real and sweaters, skirts, the reason kids worked, almost all of them after school. You could get a used car very cheap, and you could drive around in it, go to a movie with a girl in a place that looked like a large parking lot. They would marry right away, I found out later when I could speak, but nobody explained why they rushed into it. Girls, the older ones, went steady, a new word Father didn't know. It meant something like being engaged, sort of but not quite; to tell others about their new situation they wore men's rings around their necks and were always together with that person. It would take me a long time, maybe a year, to discover that my attempt to get good grades had no value whatsoever. It was sneered at; you were called 'brainy' and brainy was the least popular adjective you could be described by at Roosevelt High.

Looking good was important or at least that was how they all perceived it. For this, girls wore new clothes every day. They couldn't be caught wearing the same skirt or sweater, and they always bought more because they never had enough. All of them wanted to be cheerleaders, and they wanted to go steady with boys whose jackets they would wear. Now these boys, the objects of their desires, were rough-looking, with large shoulders and bull necks and ugly hair all shorn at the top. No matter how hard I tried, I could never find anything appealing about them. I still don't, after all these years. It's subjective, the nature of our attractions, cultural too, these football heroes, all muscle and beef, were perhaps the American counterpart of the fearless virile warrior Mother admired.

If you can't speak, and hearing doesn't help, your eyes are everything. Through them, I absorbed the world that year. Those first days at school my eyes reacted to the absence of grace, to ugliness, or to what I perceived as ugliness, which doesn't mean it really was. Blame it on the contrast — my black uniform at home, black dress with a white lace collar, quiet white halls where my feet echoed on the stone. The mood was closest to that of a church. Here, in the green halls, neon lights flickered, and there was constant noise of kids running to and fro. Girls my age had very bad skin, pimples and scars from pimples, and when they ran into the bathroom it was to put more of that goo on. It was crowded in front of the mirror in the morning. Forbidden smoke rose from the toilets. With a wet sponge they applied cake make-up all over until their faces became an even rose or chalk shade, then layers of mascara with a brush, and finally very red lipstick. Eyebrows were plucked and repainted to match their hair, which was often bleached a very pale, almost white shade. Next to them in front of the mirror I looked thin, paler than I was, because their faces had all that color. At the end of the year, my face would change somewhat, — a bright red spot where my mouth used to be. From then on, my mouth grew, became more visible, the center of attention. Before, in my memory, my eyes had been what others looked at.

In the lavatory, girls didn't look at me. I could come, look, and observe because I was not there for them or for me. My clothes didn't change every day like theirs; I wore the same old brown skirt and brown sweater, or a pleated green one with a sweater or two, that's all I had that fall. Father had to give in to brown loafers and white socks out of necessity; what else could I wear? We couldn't find wool stockings in any store. How I missed my warm stockings and my black uniform; you never had to think about dressing, that was the best part, your mind was free to wonder about other more complicated, more interesting things.

Why are they so fat, I wondered. We had no fat people at home; and girls were always thin until they got married and had a few children, but even then they were not so fat as 'zaftig'. Here, in addition to being fat, they wore their skirts tight, ass sticking out. They giggled constantly for some mysterious reason. Explosions of gum, teachers yelling "Spit it out!" and like that, all the time. All those poor frightened teachers didn't know what to do or how to behave — they were outnumbered. I couldn't figure out why kids acted that way, why their hips were so large and their walk so ungraceful except for the Negro students, who seemed to move differently, sort of gliding. Outside the school, girls wore white scarves tied under the chin, and their feet went shuffle-shuffle, small steps because their skirts were long and tight. You could never ran in such a skirt. At times, boys walked with them, looking awkward, girls' books in their hands. However, most of the time, girls walked alone and giggled uncontrollably, stupidly, in packs.

Nobody would believe me, I didn't bother writing about all this. Besides, I couldn't have done it. I was submerged in it. And then, even if I tried, I knew it would be pointless, too much, too many details to explain. Who wants to bother with so much? It was too different, it was some other world, all upside down, everything that was good before was bad now, and so forth. Here, nobody introduced you properly to anyone, they didn't hug or touch at all, yet the moment school was over, they kissed in the parked cars, in broad daylight. Dad had noticed it too. They talked about it constantly — kissing, kiss, kissed me, at school and on TV. It was most peculiar. I don't think we talked about kissing so much, but considering my lack of expertise how would I know? In my distant memory, so far away now, almost dreamt, I see couples pressed against each other in the shade of linden trees in the darkness of the park, near the river banks at night. Not us older girls. Fireflies around them. Nobody had that goo on their face, and we looked like young girls, serious in our uniforms, our faces clean. They looked like whores; Dad said that about girls from my school, but that word had no meaning yet for me, even though Mother had used it once to describe that German woman. I've never known a whore; sluts, maybe.

No, I didn't write anything sad in my letters home. Just polite short notes saying that we were doing fine and learning more every day, but if I could have said anything accurately, it would have turned into one prolonged aaaaaah! or a howl the way wolves do. I howl inside, only my mouth is mute. If at least the boys were handsomer, or even cuter. If at least they had beautiful eyes or something to make my eyes happy. Those ugly haircuts, either long with one greasy curl falling between their eyes, or short, straight up in the air like the needles of a porcupine. And all those pimples. I grew obsessed with fat and pimples, like a problem to solve. Dad says it's the food they eat, Cokes, cupcakes. He says their teeth will rot. Yes, their teeth are unusually bad for young people. Still the worst is that they don't have eyes I remember, with laughter in them, eyes that make you feel alive. Here, boys didn't even look at girls, their eyes went toward their breasts or their behinds. Maybe that's why girls have those pointy breasts, a way to attract boys' eyes.

My breasts are not pointy, they are barely there, just the way it should be at my age. I will never be fifteen again I thought at least once a week. Somebody has stolen my spring; it'll never come back. Sad how I think like an old woman, my head full of tragic thoughts. Alone in my room I stare into the mirror, I put on some orange lipstick — is this me? I exist in this. I put on earrings. I have nothing but this, my image in the mirror.

Chapter Twelve

Letters from friends — Mira, Anka, and Slava — came regularly after the first month. All the first letters began with, "I hope you have not forgotten me in your wonderful new life," and ended with, "Please remember where you came from." That summer, they worried about the exam, the big one, the most important, which would determine whether they would be able to continue their studies or would have to stop at the eighth grade. I didn't take that one because we were gone by that time, although I wouldn't have had to do it, they wrote, since I was the best in the class. Mira said that half the class didn't pass, but they could try once more at the end of the summer, those with two failing grades. If you had three, forget it. You had to repeat the whole year, and once again that horrible exam in all essential subjects but history would be the worst. Who can remember so many dates and battles and kings killing kings and all the conquests, everything you had learned in four years? I think they called it 'petit bac' in France, the grand bac' would come later, in the twelfth grade. And then the university, marvelous time, full of romance and linden trees. Mira said my name stayed on that board at the entrance, the same as before, every single year, but the book I was supposed to get went to Dara, who was next best. They thought this was fair, since I won't need that book any more. Too bad they didn't send me that book, I would have liked it more than anything. She didn't even mention which book it was. Mira, who had barely passed her exam, wrote in detail all the questions she had had on the oral and her good luck in getting Alexander the Great, and the first uprising against the Turks. For some reason, she had gone over this just the night before. For the oral, she said you reached inside this box and were killed or saved again by your luck but the written part was the same for all. There were so many disasters — Anka spilled her ink over her essay, Slava had a vomiting fit, and everybody went to the bathroom all the time. Both she and Slava were relieved not to have to think about this for the rest of the summer, not like that other half whose parents won't let them go swimming or anything. Mira, free of worries, deliriously happy, went on to write who she was in love with, who was wearing what on the main street at night and what was fashionable. Big belts, dresses cut on the bias, she wrote, if only she could have one made, ideally strapless but it wasn't likely. The main street was full of boys and excitement which spilled over to the river banks. A new boy had come from Zagreb, Slava wrote in August, you should see him, so handsome, so polite, hair parted to one side and what a dancer. Every time she appears on the main street he looks at her, maybe by the end of the summer something will happen. Slava was my best friend, we had sat next to each other from the first grade on.

His letters came too, the boy who was supposed to kiss me but didn't. We didn't even say goodbye to each other because he was away on a school trip and we left abruptly, not when we were supposed to. Everyone accompanied us to the train, an army of crying people, he was told about it when he got back. It remained unfinished for him too, he didn't see me leave, he didn't hold me or kiss me or anything. And while at home we never spoke about serious things, just films and school, we never touched once, now he began writing about love and passion you only find in some French book.

The next stage would have been that kiss, we had walked and talked almost a year. Having skipped this, he now talked about stuff I didn't know, mad kisses and embraces under a very hot sun, and I read and knew without knowing. In the heat of East Chicago, I grew feverish from so many imaginary kisses, I went over and over the last time we met, I stretched the moments until we moved in slow motion. It was a wonderful, perfect, breezy evening in May, the smell of lilac and roses from the gardens, his eyes luminous in that special light before night falls. The following day, the evening changed into night, the night grew longer, I added fireflies, and we kissed after all. It's real enough. I can smell all the smells and his smell too. I am so happy in this state, why would you ever need movies or drugs if you can imagine? I read his letters over and over again; they disintegrated from overuse.

I wrote back but not as often as he did, not two letters a week, ten pages each. I had nothing to report about my world and I couldn't write, like him, about our imaginary love. It didn't seem right. I knew it was not real, it had to remain just mine. My friends wrote about him, how he sat lonely and pale by the river, and the whole town knew about his sufferings. Then Slava met a boy at the beach and began going out with him every night. She described his eyes in great detail, while Mira said she is virtually in love with a boy who is better-looking than any movie star. I had nobody to look at or hug, just their letters for comfort. I waited for them daily. I watched for the mailman through the window, and then for an hour or two time stood still or was suspended. For every letter I wrote, he wrote ten. I didn't know how to lie.

Then even this bit of relief stopped. Mother and Dad must have had an argument or he was still under the influence of that man with red hair who preached about Judgment Day while looking at me. Even when he stopped coming, he continued to affect Dad's mind in the factory, during lunch break most likely. He told him over and over again he had lost authority over us. This sent Mother laughing, she said, "Oh you shouldn't listen to that unwashed creep, that spider web. Nobody is going to tell me how to live, I am too old for authority."

After that their bickering started, "What do you know?" he said. "Look at yourself," said she.

In the midst of their war, my letter arrived. Just as I was going to grab it then retreat to my room, he snatched it. "From now on," he said, holding my blue letter which I could tell was from him, "I'll read it first and then decide which parts are for you." He looked like an evil ghost. This was unthinkable. All those parts about kissing in the hot sun, all those words that were meant just for me.

"It's not fair. It's my letter," I said, angry, scared, and ashamed all at once. He slapped me next. My first slap from him. It should have hurt except I felt nothing at all. He had slapped some other person. It wasn't me. Nothing was me, not even those red marks on my cheek.

Mother went at him like a wildcat. She wanted to kill him, bite him, scratch him to death. "Don't you ever do this again!" she trembled, "I've raised them with blood and tears," she said, hitting him. "They are mine. You can't touch them or I'll butcher you like a pig." She used to beat us, and how, with a stick or a branch but it all stopped around twelve. And she who at home had slapped me for no reason except that she had heard that I'd been seen with that boy, she who forbade me to see him — now, she became my defender — I was to receive my letters without his meddling. Slap or no slap, I was confused, at least before I knew where she stood on everything. What was permitted. Of course, it had nothing to do with me. You could see they were only wrestling for power and she wanted to win. Or maybe it had to do with her own deceptions, her failed dreams, because she said in a half murmur, "Let her live. I was a fool. I didn't."

Letters couldn't substitute for life. I have nobody, I thought that day. She was not defending me. I cried for a long time until I had used up all the tears. A pleasant state of numbness set in. I slept for hours, uncertain if this was sleep. I wasn't hungry, I didn't want to eat. If I kept this up, I knew, or I hoped, I would just die in my sleep. That's how old people did it, and Grandma died the same way, after three days of sleeping. She simply made up her mind not to go on; she even knew the exact day she would die. At least I had a plan. It was better than nothing.

Stojan came to my room; he begged me to eat. He couldn't imagine someone just stopping. He cried, this was scary to him. He looked sad, his tears looked like huge raindrops. Mother tried to be stern like in the old days, I'd better get up and eat or I'd get sick. She didn't suffer all those years to have her daughter die of starvation in Chicago. Her mouth opened, closed, eyes flashed. I didn't move. I didn't care. Her words were just meaningless sounds escaping. The idea that maybe I was dead already and this was only a memory of the moments before passed through my head. After a certain time, which could have been hours or days, Stojan appeared again and told me that the victory was mine — nobody could ever again read my letters. I said nothing. I didn't care. Then he sat on my bed and sighed like an old woman.

This was unbearable. He needed a handkerchief, he was wiping his nose with his sleeve but tears just kept flowing silently down his cheeks. It was so sad because he still had those baby red cheeks and I couldn't stand to see him cry in a grown-up way. He only cried for reasons that were very clear — when he lost his keys, when kids beat him up. Now in front of my eyes he was turning into an old man. I got up.

My victory should have made me happy, but it didn't. Dad lost. I didn't like the look of defeat on his face now. Besides, the letters were only letters and no more. Just paper and ink. I couldn't prolong the evening with that boy forever nor could I imagine as before everything that was needed, all the details, so that in my head at least we kissed after all. I didn't want to, or I couldn't, imagine any more. I couldn't imagine the future me, my past was gone, my present was what it was, is there a word for this state? However, something of my wish to die remained in me, half-dead I kept thinking, she died in East Chicago.

Chapter Thirteen

That year, our first American year, nobody noticed when the seasons changed, when summer merged into fall and then winter arrived as harsh as the summer had been. We knew it was winter because it was very cold and heaps of black snow accumulated along the path I took to school. With snowdrifts on each side, you couldn't avoid getting splashed by the cars passing on Chicago Boulevard, humming in all seasons.

The snow in East Chicago fell differently than at home — it seemed wetter, less silent, and was dirty even before it hit the street. That's what we saw when we looked up toward the sky. Honestly, we did. Having forgotten the horrible summer, we thought this was worse, this damp snow and the wind that burned your skin, especially that portion of the leg between the sock and the skirt. You have to dress this way or they'll look at you. How I wished I could have some warm wool stockings or real boots with ski pants, which we wore in the winter, the same as the boys. For some unknown reason, pants were forbidden for girls at Roosevelt High, and everyone wore those shoes called loafers, something even the poorest peasant girl at home wouldn't wear. Not in the winter, not in the snow. At least she would have some rubber boots with wool socks to keep her feet warm. And that's not all. My pale gray coat had only one button at the top, which meant I had to hold onto my coat with one hand at all times or the wind would blow through me. Women's clothes are not made for comfort in this country, that's for sure. Why not, I kept wondering, why are the girls left to freeze in the wind? We had always imagined it otherwise. Everyone always said how Americans are practical and women so free, you can go crazy not understanding. How can you be free if you are cold? That is the question.

They fussed too much with their hair at school, it was a never-ending concern. Something was always wrong, either the color or the cut, and they must have been thinking about it after school too. Girls arrived hair full of pins which they undid in the bathroom, and then brush brush. My own hair was the same as always — long, slightly wavy, parted on one side. Besides this, I don't know how I appeared to others — sad and lonely, most likely. Was it my loneliness that provoked her or something else I did, I'll never know. The girl who was combing her hair before the mirror, whose face I now see better than my own, said all of a sudden, "Do you like America?" as I came out of the John. For once, there was no one in the bathroom except us. I had left my chemistry class to pee.

I had never seen her before; was she in one of my classes? I was prepared for her question, and I knew how to answer this one. Why didn't I simply smile and say, "Yes, I do," the way Dad said I had to answer, I should have done that instead of "so so," a gesture with my hand.

"You eat good here," she said and then she made funny sounds with her mouth while rubbing her stomach with one hand. Not knowing what to say, I shrugged; food tasted better at home, or my hunger was different, and Mother's bread with lard on top, after swimming in the river, tasted better than anything.

Was I thinking about the bread at this point, or was my face blank? She didn't like what she saw, that's for sure. She seemed angry, red in the face, she kept pointing at my skirt — then she spun me around. "Girdle, where is the girdle?" she yelled. I understood nothing until she lifted her skirt up. It was white. It covered her stomach and her upper thighs, making the flesh look squeezed. I had never seen one before. I had assumed that American asses were shaped differently, flat and straight, unmoving, but it all had to do with this contraption they wore. It didn't look comfortable, and it must be worse in the heat. Mother said they had them at home too. You wore it if you had a medical problem.

"And a bra, you don't have a bra," she yelled some more and then began poking me in the chest, pulling at my sweater. Why should I wear a bra if I had nothing to put in the bra, I wanted to say but didn't know the right words. I was frightened, I began laughing. It didn't occur to me to run.

"You are a Communist," she said next, hurling me across the bathroom. "Communist," she repeated. "My father says so." Obviously it was linked to girdles and bras. Until this year in America I didn't know Communism was so evil and dangerous. Of course Mother wasn't a Communist, but, when she said it, it meant other things, civil war, people she had lost. And then, even she who had spent time in prison soon after the war, even she said there were some good

Communists, especially the real ones, rather than the miserable little opportunists. I was a Communist the way the French are French. I was born in it, that's all I knew. Her words produced no effect on me, but I was stunned by the hatred in her eyes, and by the way she kept poking me. I wondered why she hated me so much, and for no reason? From that encounter I've always keep a certain fear when entering women's bathrooms. You never know what's lurking out there, and whenever I hear that word Communism used in a certain way, I can't help thinking, I see a girl without a girdle or a bra.

Soon after my attack in the bathroom, I went home for lunch (which virtually nobody else did) and where Mother cooked as always and Dad sat in his usual spot next to the dictionary. That day he must have been on the night shift. He helped me find the word I was looking for; he didn't ask me why I needed it. In the afternoon I told my chemistry professor the new word from the dictionary, and he was not ashamed like others that his parents were Polish. He told me this the very first day in an attempt to help me translate some words, except that I didn't understand his Polish any better than his English. Now, he didn't understand what I meant by 'offended.' Dad's dictionary didn't have a word for hurt. He got it finally, everything, bathroom, bra, girdle, and Communism. He hugged me then, and I cried loudly the way kids do, not because I was offended, but because I was lost. For a moment, with his arms around me, I am in the world, I am real, I am me. He said, slowly, "You finish school and then you escape, and be free."

Was he telling me to escape? At that moment in his arms this escape seemed real, possible — yes, I'll do it! I believed him, but not for too long. It couldn't be sustained — that was the problem. The day when I would escape seemed far, uncertain, escape to what I no longer knew. My chemistry teacher meant some other form of escape, something I couldn't know or imagine, and every minute, every day, is an eternity to a fifteen-year-old girl who can still remember that she was alive once. My life is slipping away, I'll never be fifteen again, a voice in me repeated with a vengeance. It's over, over with. Maybe I've died already and maybe it was her ghost talking to this man, learning English. It'd be her ghost who later began putting on lipstick, wearing a bra, even having good times, but none of it would be real, an actress in a play. Before that happened for good, really for good, still somewhat conscious of who I was, still me, I made one last attempt to escape like he said I should do. To me, the only real escape meant to go back home. I didn't dream about it this time. I tried it for real.

In the school library I found the phone number and address of our consulate in Chicago. Secretly I wrote them. A very simple letter. Please rescue me, I said, or I'll die. Every day I waited by the door.

They answered in a few days. They said that as a minor they would need my parents' permission, and they asked if I knew where I would live. With relatives? Without them I would have to go to an orphanage, but then my parents would have to agree. That settled it. My aunt's apartment was too small even for her and forget about permission from parents. It would only trigger another horrible fight. Fortunately nobody found out. Dad was in the factory, Mother in the basement when the letter arrived. That was it. The fight was over. I had tried. What more can you do?

Years later, among my many unanswered questions, I wondered, unable to stop about this one too — who would I have been had we stayed at home, and a similar one — what if I had grown up in an orphanage?

Chapter Fourteen

It wasn't as if the angels didn't exist, occasional good souls. Our savior came to see us, but less often in the cold weather because he could not invent a suitable activity for us. I took every bit of joy wherever it came from, I gasped for breath in silent misery nobody was aware of. My body functioned well, I was pretty, I had no pimples, I studied hard, that's why they didn't notice. Sometimes at night, I prayed to Grandma who had loved me so much and who always said she'd help me, even from her grave. To my horror, her old face began to fade, I could not conjure her up at will, and my own words to her seemed manufactured, a cover-up. She didn't want to travel all the way across the ocean, it was too far. She had never anticipated this problem when she died.

In school, it was a life half dreamt, life under water, sort of. My sweet chemistry teacher smiled at me often, he was so proud that my exams were better than anybody else's in class. He shouldn't have announced all this in front of them, all of them snickering, didn't he know better? They laughed after class too about my good grades while I only wished I could disappear or walls would absorb me somehow.

The French teacher I had met the very first day because they had sent her to interpret for me. She continued this function, and she helped by translating English words into French ones, but my French vocabulary was limited, and by the time I had translated from French into Serbian I was already two steps removed. She didn't know either that I was gasping for breath, drowning because she too wanted to be consoled about her own life, why she was in this horrible city and school, what had gone wrong and where? She used to refer to students at Roosevelt High as 'ils' and we, she and I, were 'nous'. "Ce sont des brutes," she whispered, as if afraid. She had her own tragic story, why she had been left in this dismal place, a confusing grown-up tale she could not fully explain. Nor could I understand. Her language was airy, soft, spring-like; in spite of her gloom, I realized that it's hard to communicate real despair in French. Her 'tristesse' was sweet, tender, in pretty shades of blue, lavender, maybe light gray, and the word itself had a sound of joy. My own Slavic grief was pitch-black, refused any description except oj oj, and it made things worse that in my language I didn't yet know the right word for this kind of total unhappiness. It existed only for grown-ups.

The French and chemistry teachers were the only ones who mentioned their background at school. Students with Polish or Slovak names, whose parents and grandparents were born in Europe, didn't want their backgrounds discussed. Just American, they said. Their first names were changed to John, Richard, Jane; the last ones shortened and altered. They seemed ashamed of their fathers, they refused to learn and did everything they could to forget the language their mothers spoke. They often made fun of them and me, but this has changed since then. The words America, American have changed, too, and the word Communism, and the idea that everyone in America, including Roosevelt High, was 'just middle class.' That's what they said and thought they were. Uncertain about that word 'class' for years to come, I didn't assign it to me, lower, middle, or high. Instead I used the term D.P., what they called us with mockery in East Chicago, something no one wanted to be. And while D.P sounded bad because I didn't know its meaning, the word 'Displaced Person' seems an accurate description of me.

A sudden frenzy of Christmas took over the school. On TV and radio, nothing but this, singing, jingling of bells, White Christmas, merry, merry, laughing all the way. Students at Roosevelt High actually believed that bells were invented for this date, stored up and brought out once a year, along with a tree and decorations. There was feverish anticipation in the air, the promise of things to come, a deliverance — from what? I wished it would get hold of me, too, but, stuck in my realism, I was unable to connect all those songs, sleighs, reindeer, and White Christmases to East Chicago. The color was the problem — how could they be so blind? Around us everything was gray. I had known the white snow, and my grandpa had had a sleigh with two horses and the horses had necklaces of bells at all times. In the winter we traveled all bundled up, gliding, the sound of bells, the crisp snow, the wind, and the whip merged. There is nothing like it, not even swimming. In the gray auditorium, for weeks nothing but songs about Jesus and his birth, hurry, rush, buy, not much time left. They asked me if I was getting ready and I said no, for what? No tree? No. Presents? No. Poor you, some said, some looked sad. It was hard then and now to tell them that nations, like people, have different dreams. Even when they hear it, when they get the facts, their eyes don't really accept it — poor you — only what's American is normal, get it? I was lucky I couldn't speak, and when one teacher asked me to tell the class about "my Christmas," I only mumbled and she didn't persist. Imagine if I had told them that we burn our tree the day before or about the fires to celebrate the spring — savages they'd think, and if I said that we celebrated New Year's Eve more than Christmas because all religions are the opiate of the people, they'd think that girl is crazy. They wouldn't have called me Communist because nobody read Marx at Roosevelt High, nobody, not even the teachers. I could have recited the entire Communist Manifesto — it would have been no different than reciting from a Roman poet or a Greek. Nuts, they would have said, she is just nuts. Communism in Roosevelt High had to do with not wearing girdles or bras, why would they pick on underwear I wondered, not understanding the country or them at that moment.

Still, there were kind people. Maybe I didn't see them the way I do now with the clarity that comes with age, yet the proof that they existed is that I remember them. The girl from my homeroom (I think that's what the class was called), who looked like an African princess from my dad's old books, said to me the day before the Christmas break, "This is for you." In a small box tied with a red ribbon there was a rhinestone bracelet from her mother, she said, and two small ducks from her. She pinned those two ducks on my sweater next to each other and said, "I tell my mamma about you." I'll always wonder what she had said to her mother about a girl who sat next to her in this strange class called homeroom, how did she describe me? I always wished I knew. I must have known without knowing that she liked me; maybe that was the reason I started to cry as she pinned those ducks on my sweater. She dried my tears with her hands; we didn't know others were looking at us, shocked apparently by this spectacle — black girl and white girl crying together. I heard about it much later, a proof of my Communism was in this too. I still have the ducks, the bracelet I gave in the sixties to Slava, a girl who had sat next to me in grammar school. I still wonder what happened to that girl in East Chicago whose name I am not sure of. Her face is not in the yearbook; maybe she was sick the day pictures were taken. I would love to find her but don't know how. Maybe when this book is published, I think, getting excited, she'll read and know it's her I am talking about and she'll reach me. It has happened before with my short story in Mademoiselle and it happened again with the first play; tons of people I had lost all across America found me again. She'll know it's me because of those ducks, and maybe she'll remember the sweater I gave her, the one she admired, made by my mother, a dark green cardigan with embroidery on the front. Maybe after Christmas. Mother didn't object to my giving it away, she also cried when I showed her the bracelet and the ducks. There are times I am sure her name was Ginny.

Barbara must have liked me too in her own mute way, another girl I met in my homeroom. She looked like a white horse, tall and thin, with a long face, all of her features in a straight line, and she didn't wear make-up like the others or change her clothes every day. She turned up also in a sewing class, a strange subject to study at school. I didn't pick it. They said it has to be typing or sewing or shop, which I couldn't take because it was reserved for boys. In the sewing class, in a large room full of machines and noise, we had to make a skirt from a pattern you buy at the store and a blouse with a zipper on one side. There were other girls in that class, but all their faces have been erased, and there is not much left of the woman who taught us about zippers and such. Only the buzz of those machines is still with me, electric ones you start with your foot. Barbara is still alive in me too, the only one from that class who mutely waited by my locker as the school ended around three. She liked my hair, she told me, the way it waved so gently around my shoulders. It was sweet the way she had described my hair in the way nobody had done before. Hers was the color of corn and perfectly straight. She also liked my nose and my grades. My nose was not anything special, neither too short nor too long, the kind of nose you tend to forget. Apparently, my boring, very ordinary, nose was a better nose for the fifties.

She called it 'cute,' while her own — beautiful, straight, long — she detested. My grades were a mystery to both of us. Barbara couldn't understand why 1 understood Tale of Two Cities better than the rest of them did, if I could barely speak. That was our only book that semester in English class.

Poor Miss Swatz, our teacher, was so pleased by whatever I said, she bragged about it and caused me trouble she couldn't imagine. I didn't understand why it was so hard for them and not so hard for me. I assumed their thoughts were on other things. I did not think about her, that other, half-dead girl, who leans over me as I write. She was the one who decided in advance what'd be on the biology or the chemistry exam, it's her, not me now. My grandma helped me too whenever she reached me, whenever I saw her, and then I remembered her words, "Don't cry. I won't die really." I couldn't explain all this to Barbara; I knew only a handful of the most ordinary words, but even if I had known more, I knew it couldn't be, shouldn't be done. She'd think I was out of my mind. Americans don't converse with half-dead girls or with Grandma's ghost, their thinking is thinner and straighter, like rivers without tributaries, like people you forget. I sound like my dad now; he spoke with venom.

Barbara took me home one day, to an apartment not far from us. They too lived on the second floor. Their place was not bigger than ours but appeared neater, less cluttered. No smell of cooking in the air. No lace doilies or embroidered pillows. Her mother looked like her, her father was thin and dark and his shoulders were stooped. Later, whenever I heard 'Sixteen Tons,' I thought about him. He didn't talk much about Kentucky and West Virginia where he had worked in the mines, I absorbed his life through some dust permanently stuck in his pores, so it couldn't be washed away, and it was in his lungs when he coughed. He coughed all the time, Barbara said he had an illness you couldn't cure. He never said much; maybe it was hard on his chest or he had nothing to say. He did talk about my mother's cooking; they couldn't get over it.

We invited them once, they must have been the only Americans to share our food. All three were surprised by the amount of meat we ate. They had mostly casseroles or a dish called meat pies. Our daily lunches were like special occasions for them, Barbara said, even for weddings nobody served so much. We were not rich the way she imagined; Mother simply believed in feeding us well. She used a peasant expression about how you need to feed the stomach, which in turn feeds the brain. I think she imagined that our bodies were like a furnace you need to give wood to. She also claimed that you should give the very best foods to the young. She had seen pigs and chickens grow, become plump; her concerns were with the body. She took it for granted that, if the body survived, the rest would follow on its own. She didn't worry much about our souls, or she imagined them as more flexible, less demanding, or more accommodating. In this way she was just like everybody else at home, where they always spent most of their money on food, making sure it was the freshest, the best. They licked their chops, talking about young lambs, and men compared roasts to women in their prime. Nobody ever worried about money, the fear of not having enough, not like in America where they worried all the time, and for reasons that were foreign to me. I saw stores full of food and clothes, roads full of cars, and I couldn't see where their money worries came from. At home I couldn't imagine anyone dying of hunger, we were simpler then — we would have shared, or is that called socialism? I miss that part of socialism, you didn't worry.

They were afraid of unnamed, unreal things in East Chicago. I saw the fear in the faces at school when I asked them if their parents or grandparents were Polish, Slovak, Czech, their last names had Slavic roots. No, they said, each time, I am American that's all, and they went out of their way not to learn what their grandparents spoke. They were ashamed of those weird languages, frightened that, if they said yes, I would drag them off into a dangerous, unpopular world, 'different' was the worst thing you could be, a bad, bad category. Everyone wanted to look like and have names like Jane or John and live like people on TV.

Barbara's parents were our sole attempt at friendship with Americans, but even though they invited us back once, it didn't work, couldn't. I saw it. There was a language problem and what comes with it. They mimicked, we gestured, and it was all too much work. They knew nothing about us, our history, our legends, what we took for granted, a point of reference in all our talks. Germans meant nothing to Barbara's parents, and forget our never-ending laments about five centuries under the Ottomans. What did we know about Virginia? Our temperaments were different, the reason we said they, Americans, are cold although the English are still colder. Mother's wild laughter didn't catch on. They were friendly, decent people, but somehow conquered, beaten down, and they didn't have her gift for creating imaginary good times.

Nobody did as much. She was the luckiest of all. A glass of wine produced an effect, magic of sorts; she was off to some better place we had no access to.

Who could say why I started dancing all of a sudden. Was it because I saw once again The Red Shoes! I had loved that film and the ending had always stayed with me. As far as I was concerned, the entire film was about that last line, "Please take off my red shoes" and those two in the beginning when he asks, "Why do you want to dance?" and she says, "Why do you want to live?" In between that line and the last one, nothing of importance. Middle parts never interested me much, either in life or middle class or middle age, I would always prefer the beginning or the end of things.

I began dancing, even though it was not a real dance school. The 'real one' existed far away by train and then two buses, somewhere in Chicago. I knew it was too late to start ballet at fifteen, and I had never really planned to become a dancer, it was just a dream among other dreams, like being a movie star, or a pirate, or a queen, impossible kids' dreams. In the general strangeness of our lives, it became OK to dance or to think about it as real, without any aim or ambition on my part, the same way I would do other things later on — call it freedom of the absurd.

The place was on the second floor of a building that also had a dentist, a lawyer, and a lingerie shop. The sign on the second floor said " tap, ballet, modern," and had a picture of a girl in a ponytail. To get there you took a bus, then you walked. There was only one teacher for everything, skinny old woman who looked like a bird, with a very high voice; and there was no difference between tap, ballet, or modern except for the shoes. It was a pretend school for kids to go to; it was supposed to be good for your backs and your bones.

I felt bad for the teacher, the poor woman had to pretend she knew how to move. The other school in Chicago was not only far but also expensive, so I stayed in this one. It wasn't as if she could teach me anything; that I knew. My ballet class on Saturday had a flock of kids between eight and ten, some short, some tall, some fat, and this was their first and only class. Our teacher played kid tunes on the piano, occasionally she sang. Our job was to jump around, pretending we were rabbits or birds; we were to squeal or chirp. In my half numb state I could be a part of it without thinking, less numb I would have left after that first day. Let's face it, it was not normal. I was almost grown up, much taller than the rest, and chirping like a deranged pigeon. But it was better than nothing, so I stayed. In retrospect there is something to be said for being lost — you can pass through anything because none of it matters; yet living this way gives you a way of seeing what the insane know; you are fluid, swimming in a world without borders.

After a month of these movements, the teacher suddenly became nervous, said her show was coming up and we'd better be ready. This was very important for her; it justified all her days. Why at a hospital, I wondered, aren't the patients supposed to rest? My first performance ages ago was in my town's square. It was dedicated to the Revolution, and I danced to the music from Swan Lake, directed and conceived by my gymnastics teacher from Prague. He had picked the boy for the strength of his arms and me for my feet; he always said it was a waste that I had nowhere to study ballet with feet like mine. He had also appreciated my rhythm in gymnastics to give me this big part. Now, this chirping woman wanted me to become a rabbit, and I refused to do it. I tried to tell her about my debut in Swan Lake but she didn't seem to hear it.

"If you can't be a rabbit," she kept screeching, "what can you be? Do you want to be a duck?" She herself looked like a wild turkey, and it she didn't seem to notice that I was a foot taller than those kids and I had breasts, small though. I would look silly as a rabbit or a duck.

Besides, I didn't want to be an animal of any sort.

115

'A gypsy,' I said thinking of gypsies at home and Dad's love of their tunes. She had never heard a gypsy melody, she said, but the next time she brought a record which was of a commercial variety of flamenco called Gypsy Soul. It was not what I had in mind, but it was better than the sounds of birds. Her wisdom was big — she didn't know the subject, assumed I did, and left it all up to me — to invent the costume and the steps, only the record was hers. Later, when all this seemed far away and funny, I didn't judge her harshly — she was a poor old woman, trying to live somehow, most likely she must have had the same type of lessons she gave us. In East Chicago nobody noticed, such was freedom in America.

I took my costume seriously, it was a major distraction. A skirt in brilliant colors, given to Mother on her part-time job, became my Gypsy skirt, with one end of it tucked at the waist, leaving a leg exposed. The white undershirt left my shoulders bare. Since I didn't have real roses, I tied my hair in a red scarf with a fringe, but I spent no time on the steps. I assumed it was not necessary, and we didn't have a record player.

Stojan carried my costume in a shopping bag, I remember, as we took the bus. It was spring. The black snow was melting.

I don't remember how we got into the hospital, what sort of hospital it was. Kids from my dancing class ran across the stage in twos and threes, dressed in white leotards, chirping and hopping. Then it was my turn. I let the 'gypsy passion' go for a minute, then I ran on stage, barefoot. I didn't plan my act at all, I hoped it would happen on its own, the music would lead the way most likely I wanted to be surprised myself, isn't that what a Gypsy would do? I don't know what I did, for how long, was I any good, I didn't see it, and I wasn't there. With the record turned up, I left them to swirl in the sun, somewhere in Spain, marvelous colors all around me, violent yellows, reds, and my mad passion or self-intoxication was communicated to the sick old guys who moved toward the stage, their hands extended. They tried to touch me but were restrained by nurses; from their beds they clapped and drooled sweetly. I saw them when the record stopped and I saw my teacher laugh and laugh, she was so pleased. Apparently her show was a big success, we made the patients happy. She told me they wanted it again but a few changes in my costume would be necessary. I said no, not again. My gypsy passion was over. If only I had not seen them. Closer up, they seemed so unbearably sad, much worse than I was; even if I wanted to, I couldn't invent my Gypsy joy for them again. And soon my dancing lessons stopped.

Chapter Fifteen

Our stove started acting funny one evening in March, either because we did something wrong it just decided to give up. We were alone, Stojan and I, as the stove began to smoke in a peculiar way. I waited for it to pass but it only grew worse, and then a blue smoke enveloped the kitchen. In the living room, Stojan turned the fan on, and placed it in front of him; without saying a word, deeply involved, he continued to watch what sounded like a Western. The stove grew red and sounds came out of it, like grunts. The first flames were an orange-red color, long thin snakes, beautiful to look at. I did. The first real fire since we left home. It was raining outside, with a strong wind, a pleasant sound to fall asleep to. Stojan didn't move. Bang, bang went the Lone Ranger, then he galloped off on Silver with the music in the background.

I moved finally. I didn't know what to do. Water didn't help and the window was stuck. The old man next door was not there. His dog was. There were clothes all over the floor, beer bottles stacked like a tower. There too, a TV was on: I love Lucy. His dog looked tired or old. He didn't move or bark. He was watching I Love Lucy without blinking. The lights were not on in the apartment on the first floor.

The cold air on the street woke me up. I ran to the bar on the corner. They were watching something there too and didn't hear me when I said fire. I had to shout fire! Fire! loudly, fire! I repeated, and two men jumped off their stools.

When we came in, the stove was completely enveloped in flames, flames were shooting up, eating up the wall behind the stove but in the living room Stojan still sat in the same spot with that fan which made smoke swirl above his head while he remained free. He didn't move, didn't notice any of it, the smelly stuff they poured, and all the mess. The men extinguished the flames, but the stove was gone, the landlord said it couldn't be repaired. He had to get us a new one and raise our rent.

Stojan must have been in a bad way, both of us were, except I couldn't see me. He seldom spoke now. He was almost mute. I couldn't see his thoughts; maybe he had none. We were doing what animals do, hibernating half-asleep, waiting for spring to arrive. We didn't talk about it, there was nothing to say, and we wouldn't have known what words to use. If only we had had the books, that would have been good for all four. You couldn't escape with an American book if you had to look up words every minute or so, and our dictionary had no translation for sexy or baby or cool. In addition, we were confused all the time, so confused I laugh about it now.

Mother, in her never ending optimism, claimed that America has its good sides. "Look," she said, "they love kids here more than anywhere else in the world, see, all the songs on the radio, on TV, are about their children." Yes, they were. Baby, baby, how much I miss you baby, oh baby, why did you leave me, I think about you all the time. Father should have known better, but on this issue he was totally uninformed. Consequently, we listened to those songs and imagined American love for their kids, how sad they were (maybe a baby had died, or there was a divorce) and here they were, their parents, all alone missing them. Mother said only a woman could write these songs because men.... But I was further confused when a man on the street whistled at me and said, "Baby, hey, baby!" I didn't know what to think, did I look like a baby? And why was he whistling?

We misunderstood everything including Father's popular magazines. An article in Mademoiselle gave this advice to young girls — when you have your period, you'll feel better if you have plenty of sleep, eat an apple, buy a new belt or wash the old one. Since I slept a lot and ate apples, all I had to do was wash that belt. I wanted to feel better in general. I only had one belt for everything, a black plastic one with a paper lining which disintegrated when I washed it. It never occurred to me that this elastic thing for sanitary napkins was also called a belt. Mademoiselle also had its own ideas on beauty, different from the girls at Roosevelt High. They called it the 'well-scrubbed look', very confusing. To scrub the floors OK, but your own face and with a brush? Every day too.

Mother thought they had made a mistake, you should wash your face with water and no more. How could these old women call each other 'girls' if a girl was supposed to be young? And what exactly is a teenager? We didn't even have that word or the concept; it was American only. Fine, you say, between thirteen and nineteen, it's the same as adolescent, it means the time you are neither a kid nor a grownup, but what about all the rest? Our adolescents behaved the same as everybody else, they didn't chew gum or drink endless bottles of Coke or have fits. Am I not a teenager? In these magazines, teenagers were a special group, like a nationality, and they only liked to be with their own kind. Then they ate cupcakes, gallons of ice cream, and chips while playing those unpleasant records. They bought and used Clearasil all the time. The parents had lot of trouble with them, either because their rooms were sloppy or because they spent too much time driving around. My room was clean, I didn't like Coke, and I behaved the way we were all expected to — with respect toward older people. How was I a teenager then? Why would you have children if you lost them so fast at thirteen? It looked like teenagers never went out with their parents, were ashamed of them, yet parents accepted all this as natural. With all of our communal intelligence we couldn't figure it out — because it was new to us — that it was a marketing job which created the concept which then became the norm and was then discussed, written about as a universal truth, eventually exported abroad along with other things. This way you could have magazines for teens, television programs and records and movies, one whole country to sell to, to confuse first, then to tempt. And all the books about them and for them. I had never read a teen book, it was taken for granted we would understand the other ones and because of it we did.

Mother fell in love with Liberace because she said he loved his mother more than anyone, that's a good son for you. Predictably, Father didn't see much good anywhere, he continued to read the papers and argue with the U.S. "It's nobody, not nobari," he repeated, furious the way they pronounced this word in Chicago. "Did you hear how they pronounce Arkansas?" he would shout. His rage against the spelling continued, and for a reason. Just look at the word 'through'. Our language was phonetic thanks to a marvelous reformer whose motto was, 'write the way you speak'. We had no problems with spelling, it didn't exist as a subject you teach. Spelling contests on TV didn't impress us, Dad only sneered, how dumb, how dumb. He proclaimed that after he was done with his big work, American kids would suffer less. He would simplify everything, no spelling problems or illogical prepositions. In addition to receiving their gratitude, he expected to cause a big stir. He rejoiced in imagining the surprise, then the rejection, until everyone finally admitted he was right after all. The book was to be called, One Man's Fight for Logic in English.

A serious unreality settled over us. Mother started painting her toenails to spite him and she moved her toes provocatively in a way I had never seen. This was her rebellion because she knew he didn't like red toenails. He said they were vulgar and she looked like a waitress. On the other hand, she refused to shave her legs or armpits like American women; she didn't care if people made fun of us; at home body hair was sexy. She didn't say sexy since we didn't have that word, she said appealing. That word sexy reached Yugoslavia later, along with the rest in the seventies, I think. Come to think of it, that word 'sexy' was confusing to us even though we translated it as 'attractive, appealing American style'. I was confused about why it had to do with breasts so much, the big ones, why the women who had them were sexy. That word didn't apply to men for some reason, it was less clear how men were supposed to be appealing, what they were supposed to have. Whatever it was, it was more mysterious, less obvious than breasts. And then we were confused even more because most women they called sexy in those magazines didn't appeal to us — they were doll-like and yet metallic, and their breasts pointed sharply. "You don't want to dance with a woman like that," Dad said, "she'd poke you."

Chapter Sixteen

My town left me bit by bit. When I tried to, I couldn't see it or smell it. Not well. I was no longer sure it was my town or some other place I had imagined. Grandma's face appeared less and less often; when I tried talking with her something stopped me, I had nothing to say or I didn't know how. English didn't seem right and my own language felt strange. She didn't want to see me any more, I guess. I had forgotten what words I had used, how I addressed her. It wasn't 'Grandma' I called her — it must have been something sweeter, just for her. As a replacement for everything, I began going to Saturday night Elks dances; Barbara didn't want to go alone. She didn't say why she wanted to go so much if we got bored the very first time. In that large hall on a large empty dance floor a few 'steady couples' always clung to each other, in a slow dance. Others — girls on one side — giggled and rushed to powder their noses in the bathroom, boys stood in a pack, pacing nervously, slugging each other, uncertain what to do with their arms and feet. They appeared encumbered by their bodies, ill-at-ease like wearing a dress that's not yours and too large. Is this sweet sixteen? The boys didn't ask girls to dance, Barbara said, because most of them didn't know how.

After these dances, the loneliness in me was worse than anything. Sometimes, unnoticeably I saw my old friends dancing, kissing, laughing, but only once in a while. The loneliness snuck up, unpleasant all of it, while Barbara and I walked home alone, on the edge of the boulevard. I see us now — we are two girls in blue-and-green skirts made in sewing class. I see us from the back while the cars move toward me at full speed, and all that noise prevents me from hearing what we are saying. Maybe we said nothing. She was silent too.

It was always like that, but I never said no. But this one time at the Elks, on a Saturday night, the mood was different from the beginning. Even my skirt was special, a very clingy black rayon, slit on one side, with a black jersey tucked in, and I wore gold earrings you get at the dime store. I think Silvana Mangano wore a similar costume in Anna and Mambo, two films which left their feverish mood in me. I didn't know how I looked, what effect I would produce; up to this year I had been a proper girl in uniform, so what is this clingy black skirt? I didn't buy it, that's for sure; somebody gave it to Mother for me; it fitted beautifully, like a dance skirt. If I saw her now, this girl, this other me, I would think mostly of French films of the sixties full of nymphettes with small breasts, in bare feet. Even now, years later, I almost see her eyes that night, mad eagerness dying for something to happen, anything exciting. I didn't know what that would be nor how to look for it, even the word exciting was brand-new for me.

A surprise at the entrance. A real band was playing. They were young, unusual-looking, their faces various shades of brown and gold, and their music was nothing like the jukebox on other Saturday nights. They laughed while they played, their teeth gleaming, their arms strong, they were so exciting to look at, but for some reason there were no white students on the dance floor.

"I don't know how, I can't," Barbara said, when I asked her to dance with me. It was the first time I had wanted to, in me there was an urgency, a need you can't describe with words, call it a wish to explode. It was the happiest music ever, red, purple, deep blue, and you heard the ocean roar in the drums. Back and forth it went hitting the shore. I wanted to dance at that moment the way you want to eat or drink, it didn't matter that I didn't know how, who I danced with. How did I grab her, that sweet girl who gave me those ducks, I don't remember, nor the moment I pulled her to the dance floor. Then time stopped and we went far, with drums going I was sure, anything could happen, maybe I would embrace the sun. How I guessed the steps I don't know, they were given to me by the drums. I know this — they were not mine, and my legs, shoulders, hips belonged to some other girl who then went on to dance possessed while the band broke all the rules and didn't stop. Around us, as in a dream, a blur of faces, clapping, go baby, go, red, sweaty, mouth open, the drummer's hands were amazing, tam tam tam, his eyes laughed tam tam and Genny must have been a princess in Sudan and I God knows who. Mrs. Winters knew who she was because she pulled us apart roughly hurting my shoulder. She looked mean, angry, a missionary with a silver bun. Then everything went dead. The music had stopped. I understood nothing except that my dance was over, and that once again I was in East Chicago. The band was packing. They were told to leave —why? The drummer, who had the nicest gold skin and very beautiful teeth, whispered, "Baby, you have guts." I didn't know what he meant by guts.

Walking home on the boulevard, cars buzzing, my body throbbing, dancing still, music in my head, something unfinished in my arms, I asked Barbara about 'guts'. Is it good or bad? what is it? I wanted to know. She said it was good, then told me she was surprised. She didn't know I was a dancer. I didn't either I said, but maybe I am. To Slava I wrote, "It's a strange country. Here you just do things suddenly and then that's what you are."

That word 'guts' bothered me. Barbara didn't really explain. In the dictionary it said stomach or entrails which made no sense. How could it be good? I wondered. Later somebody told me it was the same as 'you have a lot of balls,' which was equally strange if you were a girl. Dad didn't know what it meant either but he didn't care since the American way of speaking had no logic. "Imagine this," he said raising his finger. "They tell a pretty woman that she looks like a million dollars. So stupid! Who ever saw a million dollars and it's only paper? They should say *You look like a flower or a sunny day.*

"When did you ever call me a flower?" Mother says.

"I did. You forgot."

"No," she says, "you called me a healthy horse."

And they started arguing again. What a nightmare! Where did I land?

Then he went on to talk again about his book and how everything would change once it was written. I didn't tell him or her about my dance. It couldn't be told to anyone, it was a brief moment of passion. It was better than watching Mangano in Anna and Mambo.

I didn't sleep that night, burning up, full of music that had nowhere to go. Not much of this remained the following day except a sensation, a memory of a dance half-dreamt, but unfortunately it stayed with them at school, and all those who hadn't seen me dance talked about it, while those who had, magnified it and my dancing continued to excite them after it had stopped. To dance the way I did was apparently forbidden, and that was why I had guts. At the same time, I didn't understand the reasons for their excitement or the proscription, it was only a dance, and it was over. In the halls, boys now whispered at me in passing, words I didn't know, and the looks they threw in my direction were confusing — fear, shame, curiosity, all mixed up. Girls averted their eyes intentionally; up to now, I hadn't even existed for them. They were now letting me know they didn't like me, that much I could tell.

Another group began watching me too — black students communicated some other, almost a family, feeling which was never expressed in words. From their eyes I gathered warmth, the way they moved or laughed was closer to home, and I began thinking that some Americans were attractive after all. Like all early friendships or loves this was simple and ordinary; they helped me live, I suppose. I am using that word 'black' now, not knowing what else to say. At the time I didn't think black or Negro but coffee, honey, chocolate, or the girl with braids, the boy with golden eyes.

Miss Winters, whom I hadn't known until now, was watching me in a way that was not kind. Her eyes carried a menace of sorts, I avoided her as much as possible. She was tall, thin, her mouth a straight line with no lips, and eyes of slate gray matching her name and her suits. Her function as a girls' counselor was unclear to me. Barbara said it had to do with punishment and discipline for the most part. This left me puzzled — were there different rules for girls, were they punished differently? We didn't have anything similar at my old school, nothing so specialized.

My chemistry teacher was watching me too. I would raise my head and he'd be looking at me. He had large brown eyes, and was sort of round, chubby, like a teddy bear, the kind of person you think of as your uncle. The way he looked at me was peaceful, really nice, I imagined he wanted to give me a hug. One day he led me out of the class into an office where a man gave me a test which resembled a game. All you had to do was match some pictures and rearrange triangles, circles and squares; there was nothing to write; I didn't say a word. A week later, the same chemistry teacher took me out of the class again and announced in the principal's office that I could graduate right away. He was so happy about this, so proud, while my first thought was, oh God, now I'll get cheated out of high school too. In the hall he said, "You had French, you had math, go to college next year. Go. I am afraid for you."

Again I understood nothing. Afraid of what? He couldn't explain, but this was a warning. At home they were confused too. I couldn't leave the following year, Mother said. I was too young to go away. We had no money for it, not yet. In a year, she said, with her part-time job, we'd have enough. However, she more than anybody else saw this event as a cause for celebration, a good story, a proof that I was better than others, and, since I was her daughter, obviously it all had to with her. She bragged and bragged, everyone heard about it, nobody was skipped. At school everyone knew about me from then on. It was an unprecedented event at Roosevelt High, a student from behind the Iron Curtain skips two grades and she could have even skipped three.

The school paper wrote something about IQ, the meaning of which was foreign to us, then later an East Chicago paper exaggerated everything to include my struggle against Communism and how happy I was to be in a free country. These were supposed to be my words. I never said such a thing. I still have that bit of paper and my picture in a black sweater, dime store pearls around my neck. The paper also said how I was an accomplished dancer, and this stayed in my head, what if I was? At school they were confused too — they liked me as a dancer, they could imagine it, it was on TV and films, but now I was called 'a brain' in the halls, not a good thing to be especially if you are a girl. "How could you be a brain and a dancer?" a boy said in my chemistry class, "it ain't natural." Football players said horrible things to me now, judging by their expressions, was it hate I saw? The front door was the worst place in the morning when they stood on each side jeering, whistling, and I had to squeeze through this narrow corridor without being touched. I hated them but there was nothing I could say or do. I didn't even know the right words. "I hate you" would have been too small and inefficient.

Chapter Seventeen

That year the spring was not very different from the fall in any way. Only when the dirty snow disappeared for good and was replaced with dust, did I see with horror that a year had passed.

Was this the reason why I did what I did, the awareness of time I couldn't stop? In retrospect, one can say this or that, pinpoint a cause but none really fit and everything paled in comparison with real life, because we don't fall in love with Mr. X because he is A plus B and we don't wish to die because of a D plus F. Only people outside the situation can calmly lecture oh how sad, oh, it's because she didn't have enough friends, and her family was strange, and she failed to adjust, or they should have talked more about it. Some wouldn't understand any of it because it goes against all the usual pragmatic reasons, and the optimistic approach to life that a girl who is pretty, 'winning,' skips two grades and has every reason to rejoice — that she would even think about death. They would then look for all sorts of childhood traumas and would be wrong. That girl would have never considered anything similar at home, not even in thought, but did it because of something in the air of East Chicago. Whatever fragile life there was around me wasn't enough, to understand the reasons you would have to feel the same loss, except there is no adequate word for it really. Death is still the best.

I do remember days before or maybe it was more like a week. A certain clarity of scenes dreamt. Lunar lights. We took a train to Chicago, Mother and I, so she could talk to some woman whose cousin she knew at home. She had to talk to another woman, she said. It's May. There is music somewhere on the lake, drifting from a boat in the marina. I hear this music in the apartment where these two gab and I sit. Either I imagine or I really see young girls in white dresses moving gently to the sound of a waltz, and I know even then that real life is not what I have, me, watching them, nor will I ever live it nor will it ever be possible. I will never catch up. I have lost a year, I keep thinking, a whole year. My sad sixteen-year-old body which was supposed to change a bit has refused to. My breasts haven't grown any bigger, my hips remain the same, the same as at fifteen. I have not kissed anybody yet and when I do it, it will already be too late, because it's simply late forever, I kept thinking, watching those girls move on the lake late at night. I will always be somewhere else, but at that moment in May I am broken. It's the small moments like that that count. The music and those girls are intolerable. It's moments like that that kill you, it's not what you think. I know more on this subject than the experts. After all, I tried it, didn't I?

When I crawl into her skin now, it's scary. I never stay long, I worry. She is in a void, she is not there. I exist in the objects — dresses, lipsticks I put on, but my image in the mirror is not me. Oh no, I would know. Why do I keep on putting those lipsticks on, a patch of color, bright red, pink. For no reason, just to see. To see what? To see who she'll become, that girl. That spring, as the new wave of heat began, I am not sure I am alive, you could prick me with a needle and nothing would happen, nothing, just blood. I do this sometimes, in secret, fascinated by the color red on pink. Even the heat I feel less this time. It's not like last summer. This heat is less hot. I can't understand why the fan is on when my stomach is like ice.

I remember this moment: the old man yelled something. I heard the dog squeal. The smell of the factory came through the windows, sharp, acrid, mixing with the smell of our dust. It was the same smell as the day we arrived. Nothing was left of my previous smells although I knew they were shrubs and roses. When I tried to see Grandma, her face wouldn't come up, and the words I had used to talk with her or pray to her were gone completely. The silence enveloped me from inside. The apartment in the yellow light had the clarity of something seen for the first time and full strength I got it — everything shabby, dusty, already worn, in ugly shades of green, green sofa, green carpet, how could it all be so worn in a year, how could it be so green, I kept thinking. Then once again I felt the heat, it would be a repeat of last summer. We had skipped the spring. If it happened, nobody saw it, not me, it went by, maybe for a week. Strange how we skipped it.

I am alone. I like it this way. Dad is on his night shift, Stojan and Mother have gone to visit someone, might not come back until the next day, isn't that what she said? Yes, sure, the trains stop around midnight, she said not to worry. I am definitely alone. A pleasant sensation. I've always loved being alone. As a child, I escaped that way, hypnotized by the treetops and moving clouds. In the kitchen that night I escaped again — for a few seconds I saw our old place on the ground floor, the smell of lilac in the air. I was on the main street too, cool in the month of May, and my friends were promenading up and down and tomorrow they'd go swimming at my favorite spot below the falls, where the water is transparent and so clear you can drink it.

I drank it. The joy I knew was immense. The river was in me, around me, I could smell it.

Then the dog howled again. The pain I felt next cannot be named. Nothing as big as that exists in English or any other language. It can't be explained well, it was my entire body that hurt. On TV, the Colgate commercial was on, advertising that special ingredient which like an invisible shield protects you from cavities.

131

The man threw something at the dog, a beer can? In the mirror, I didn't see myself any more, it was some other girl who went toward the stove, opened the oven, turned the gas on for baking and all the top ranges too, made sure the windows were shut, and calmly got into bed.

He said casually in the morning, "I have told both of you that you have to light the gas with the match, don't forget it the next time. You left the gas on." He showed again how to do it. He looked tired, gray in the face, unshaven. I was neither happy nor unhappy. He had come in time to open the windows. I don't remember the last night well. The need to die is as violent at sixteen as the need to live but it was a temporary violent desire, done on the spur of the moment. And yet it was real — I wanted to disappear. It was so strong and urgent it didn't even occur to me to leave a note, a goodbye letter, something. It was as strong as hunger or thirst. And then I forgot it altogether.

The pain sank in deeper, was no longer expressed or isolated. Soon, that year, I would stop writing letters home for good. To function, to be, to live, I became someone else or split myself the way it happens in madness, and only later, much later, in my thirties, I couldn't figure out why I kept dreaming about a girl I had killed and nobody knew about the murder except me.

PART TWO

Chapter One

Instead of disappearing, as I must have wanted to do, I was sent to a church camp for two weeks where we swam in a lake and a young boy kissed me under water. I don't know how Mother found out about this place which had a Serbian cemetery with only a few graves, and many trees, a vastness of grass. Since that time, the cemetery has taken over and seems to be spreading, and the graves are bigger than before. We didn't pray or go to church at that place even though it was a church camp. I don't think my people are too keen on religion in general. It was mostly eating, sleeping, swimming at the lake where that kid had the nerve to kiss me like that. I didn't consider what he did under water as anything real, or my first kiss because of his age and my own idea of what the first kiss was supposed to be. This, under water, didn't feel like anything, it wasn't as good as kissing a friend on the cheek. He had been a sweet chubby boy with very round blue eyes, unaware that I was older than him, a girl who had suffered already. "Gee," he said, eating the puff cakes and strudels, gee all the time this or that. He had been born in the States; that's why he said 'gee' so much. He kissed me only once. I avoided him after that, especially under water.

In the camp I emerged into a pin-up, what they called a 'sweater girl' even when you wore no sweater. Maybe it had to do with my red cotton top which I wore in a European style tucked inside my slacks, with a belt, and this struck them as provocative, sexy they said. They were all Americans except for Stojan and me. They said sexy too much. To this day I don't understand why a woman's body is a provocation of sorts, nor the response to it often, aggression, a suppressed hatred. I didn't understand in the same way the physical sensation of racism, still don't, but I must have my own brand of fears that Americans can't know even when they know me.

That summer some decision was made, unconsciously, like a wave washing over me — not to take anything seriously ever, to enjoy myself no matter what. The moment a serious thought appeared either about the future or the past, I squashed it. I was afraid of where it would lead, what gloom it would produce. Live now, someone whispered in my ear. That's all there is. This day this August is the only one like this, a voice in me repeated. Later, in college, my first course in existentialism was easy; I knew it already, Sartre and Camus were like old friends. They too disliked 'esprit de serieux', what's all this talk about the future. Planning for what?

We traveled with the savior that summer. Once again, he came to tempt us with sun and water. He bought me all sorts of clothes now, cotton dresses, skirts, blouses, and an expensive bathing suit in lavender shades. I could have much more, he said, if I didn't have a boyfriend. He asked me half-jokingly one day at the beach, and I said yes. Such was his demand, a form of bet, and a promise I was supposed to keep. It was easy. A boyfriend? Me? Who is there? Even that name boyfriend sounded unreal. The only boy in the entire school I liked to look at was a champion wrestler who had coffee-colored skin and very, very beautiful eyes. He moved beautifully too, like a panther. By then, after a whole year in America, I knew he couldn't ask me out. It didn't occur to me to ask him; it wasn't done. I had dresses instead, blue ones, red, green.

We went to Michigan to see the Indians who turned out to be very different from films or books, not tall, muscled, and brave, but toothless and drunk. We didn't want to believe it, we kept thinking that somewhere else further West they'd turn out fine, if only we went to Arizona, to Wyoming. I have to say that a part of me was wounded by their condition, the way they looked, the other part of me saw it as natural, I was no longer the same, why should they be? Dad didn't come with us, even though he could have. He had a week off for his vacation but he decided to keep working and make twice as much money that week. That's what most people around him did. Nobody spoke about trips or vacations in my school. It was considered a luxury, they didn't take it for granted.

We swam in all sorts of rivers that summer and ate huge steaks whenever we stopped in the evening. Our appetites were good. The savior paid for everything, motels, steaks, anything we wanted. By the time Mother reached for her purse, it was too late either because she was too slow or he was faster. However, Mother didn't feel bad about this, she said to him, "What do you, an old goat, need the money for?"

He answered her in kind, he called her an old mare. That's how they teased each other without getting angry. She was happy in Michigan, laughing, eating, she loved to see us swim, that's what summers should be for, kids, she believed. In the evenings, after dinner before I went to bed, the savior took hundreds of pictures of me, in color for the most part. They were not the usual snapshots, but posed, with lights — my legs extended, toes pointed like a ballerina, and I look shy and yet daring in the bathing suit in shades of lavender he had helped me pick out. Sometimes I would be sitting on a table covered with oilskin cloth, or I would be lying on the pillows in the strangest contorted positions which he hadn't asked for. It was my doing. The man we called the savior remained honorable in every way, in words and gestures, even when he was taking pictures of me his eyes were the same as always. His pictures were not lewd but strange, he was only documenting what he saw. In these photos my body is childish and slim, my face sweet, only my eyes are grown-up and absent, the kind of eyes I'd see on junkies later on. I would be staring ahead toward faraway planets, my gaze far far away from earth.

You learn to live with unreality, it's another kind of life. In this restful state everything is miles away, nothing interferes, sounds are less sharp, a whole portion of you is locked up tight, you are weightless, like a bird, like a plane, flying, just passing through. Without all that extra stuff to pull you toward the earth, you are so much freer than most people, and for a reason. There is nothing to lose, you aim for nothing and only this nothingness is real. Even Niagara Falls where we went on our second trip, didn't wake me up. All that thundering water was like a film of water. I saw it. I went under the falls calmly, what's the big deal? That film with Marilyn Monroe was somehow more real than the real falls. Here too he took many pictures of me in front of the falls, in front of some rose garden, in my black pedal-pushers and a white t-shirt. Decked out like this, white ballerina slippers on my feet, I look twelve except for that pose every time. While he was photographing me, other men wanted pictures of me and with me. Why? Mother didn't say no to them, or rather she said neither no or yes. I said, "Sure, why not?" She was not real either, she wondered why would anyone want a picture of this kid, she couldn't see me or understand what they were imagining. For the pictures they wanted and the ones the savior took I posed automatically as if trained — one leg over the other, chin up, eyes very wide open, a bit surprised. There are no regular snapshots of me during that time, just these horrible copies of some movie magazine acted with perfection — a girl who was once the best in school was fast at learning this too, did it well, this posturing, a form of adjustment. To what?

Chapter Two

A new man knocked on our door, he said his relatives had written to him about us. His name was Mihailo, but he said we should call him Mike. He was not like the other men around us — he spoke English, he drove the prettiest all-white convertible, and he lived differently — work during the day, university at night. Work hard, play hard; he said his weekends were his. His past was different too, he deserted from the army soon after the war, and then he had been in the American army doing something he called intelligence which neither we or he seemed to understand. Father said of course he is intelligent but it's not something you mention the first day you meet. He was younger than the others, old as far as I was concerned, with wrinkles on his forehead and around the eyes. Thirty-five, Mother thought, then said a man in his prime. She liked him because he loved to eat and laughed all the time.

Stojan and I liked him as much and for the same reasons, everything he said was funny, and he took us to drive-ins to eat. He ordered a sausage called a dog, a hot one, a new food for us, and so was the liquid ice cream you drank with a straw. Was it a soda or a shake or a malt? Every time he came, we laughed. He had a real gift for describing people, imitating our poor countrymen, how they walked on Chicago streets, the clothes they wore. "Just look at the ties," he said, "you'll recognize them this way, they always pick the loudest ones and with birds." He then told about a family he had seen, dressed in wool all three, and the father had a huge red parrot on his tie. We laughed so much about this family, forgetting that we too walked just like them on Sunday afternoons, the highway on one side.

No, he was not like the others. He had absorbed some other way of looking at life, an optimism of the American kind, foreign to us. He advised the following — get away from all those immigrants as soon as you can. Move on. Here in America you can become anyone you wish. He was impressed by my grades, I was bound to succeed even though that word 'succeed' was and would remain foreign to me.

Mike introduced some other America into our lives with his white car, his shirts without ties, and Mother, forever ready for the imaginary good times, was infected by his optimism. New unlimited horizons, bright future, my eventual success — she drank it up. She didn't understand his view of success either because it didn't exist as an idea at home where it was all finished once for all, was meant to last forever, like a woman who marries well or a man who gets a good job. She never understood the temporary nature of this American-style success or the reasons why people would go to school after that first degree and the first good job. However, she was inflamed, seduced by the word success, and who knows how she imagined it or if she did but the other part that went with it — speed and moving about, remained foreign to her always. In fact, she wanted everything old to remain the same, all the traditions and so forth and you just add success to it, making it a bigger and better version of the old life. Still, she was younger than I was. Mine was a very old view summed up by my grandfather, "What's the rush to get anywhere when you end up the same, just dust." I didn't think like this every day, of course not, just a sentence in the back of my head, a guide, preventing me from going overboard about how wonderful how great life would become, or getting carried away with the words victory, success, and so on. The reality of death always produced a nice, calming effect on me — why rush.

However, for Mike, Mihailo, I was not just a pile of dust. Even though he took us out for those hot dogs, he looked at me, just me, more and more often with that special look I would recognize in men later on. Not then, not quite. For me he was just a funny guy who took us to the drive-ins and made all of us laugh. Funny how thirty-five is too old for a girl of sixteen, even twenty-five would have been. Still, somewhere in me, I also knew without admitting it that both Mike and the savior came to see us because of me, and never, by pure miracle, at the same time. I also knew without knowing that she was letting it all happen because all of us could go out for a drive, or to the beach. She was included in everything and who could blame her for this short escape from our dreariness. It was good for Stojan too, it was a good communal decision, but how could she let me, I kept wondering, not knowing everything but some, how could she do it, she who didn't even let me go out after ten with my girlfriends and let's forget about David, forget about even seeing him on the street and forget about walking with him, the slap in the face I got — how could she then, I ask you, let this man twice my age take me out alone, in his car mind you, and never ask for details. She didn't say come back before ten, the way she should have, or where are you taking her? I am stubborn in my memory, I have had to be, it's the only thing I have as a guide. In this new country with humid hot summers and no springs, with winters that are harsh, my mother was not my mother any more with her old discipline. My mother was adjusting. She was paying him for the family fun with this evening he could be alone with me, I concluded, thinking at the same time no, it can't be true.

Later, much later when attempting to see us, that place and that time, I tried to understand her separately from me in order not to judge her harshly. Over and over again that new word 'survivor' comes up. I don't like the word too much, it's overused, but I can't think of any other as good. She would have survived anything, not me. To live was the main call, are you perhaps born with this drive, is it a curse or a gift? She could always cling to every bit of life around her, drink it the way desert plants do, store it, tell stories with it, and maybe it was just as well she let him take me out, maybe it was better that way for everyone including me. He was not evil, she could tell that much. Maybe she thought he was better than nothing, that's all. Hers was the most ordinary peasant thinking, nothing romantic or fancy, just do what you can if you can't do more.

Sweet sixteen, he called it. Sweet sweet he hummed. Why sweet, why is sixteen sweeter than fifteen, what about seventeen I wondered. They talked about it so much at school. He said it's an important birthday for a girl in the States, you had to celebrate it, everyone does so, later you would remember how sweet you used to be. So here we are out driving in his white convertible Studebaker, on a very warm night by the lake. The wind is warm too, everything is. In front of us far away very tall buildings stand erect, thousands of windows lit. Chicago by night. Blue gray and gold. The water on the lake glistens on my right, further away total darkness where water and air merge and this combination of the dark lake which shimmers, makes me think of A Place in the Sun based on An American Tragedy; but I am not sure whether I am Elizabeth Taylor or Montgomery Clift. They are in a convertible too, and it's summer. Far off, from some boat in the marina the music drifts, soft tropical sounds, rumba, merengue, gentle, persistent, and I must imagine that I really see those girls in white dresses moving, dancing, madly in love, while I observe it all from this car in motion, yet I participate in their dance too. Am I wearing white? Maybe. I don't remember either the color or the cut of my dress or anything else about me. I don't remember him any better. Only the world outside us is clear.

Our first stop is on Rush Street. A club with a piano. My first drink has cherries in it. The second one makes me laugh for no reason. I am inside a film, a light comedy, and everything is pink, cheerful, what Americans call fun. Fun time. The word and the mood are American

141

only. Lightness without shadows. That's how I see them, some words are purple, others red or green. The light mood doesn't last because we get up, go on to our second stop. We are on a street with bars and more bars, neon lights, and very sharp sounds, laughter, squeals. Girls, girls, girls, lights blink. How about this one, he says. I shrug. We are in.

It's dark at first, then very red red walls. The smell of stale beer, old clothes, old carpets, smell of old old dust. On the walls, pictures of women in feathers grin at us, and men red in the face shout from their seats, their eyes shiny. They were not young but appeared very shook up, excited by something that was bound to occur on the stage, which had dark red curtains. Mike ordered another drink for me with cherries on the top. I liked the drink; it tasted like vanilla ice cream!

A man came on stage in front of the red curtain and told jokes. Men jeered. It must have been funny. A guy next to me made motions with his arm pushing in and out like he was hitting someone. Then, as if in answer to everything he was doing, a drum was heard and the first woman appeared in a coat, a hat, and gloves. She took off her hat, or rather she threw it off the stage toward the men in the first row. She said she was too hot. This caused a lot of commotion around us. "Give it to her," men shouted, waving their fists. They seemed angry at her. Why? Next she removed her gloves slowly while the drum kept going, and men kept yelling things in her direction, their faces ugly. Off went her dress and her other glove. She kept her feather scarf and her panties but her bra she threw toward us. A man near us caught it, sniffed it, and then had a fit — at least that's what it looked like. Another guy snatched the bra and put it on top of his head, and then another one grabbed it. The woman's breasts had stars on the nipples, and she shook them left and right, looking pained. It was terrible the way she looked, how she suffered. I wondered why we were there, maybe he had made a mistake, maybe he hadn't known what awaited us. I didn't ask him. It was too noisy to have a conversation. The woman had huge monster breasts, and she kept doing things to them. Then she left.

With no rest in between, the man announced Lola, the sex queen. After a year, that word sex was still confusing. We have one like it, but it means gender; you use it for everything — people and plants. You could not say gender queen. Is there such a thing as sex king? All in all, I didn't understand much and queen Lola didn't look like a queen. She was tall and leathery and resembled an old horse, like the ones Grandpa had in his stable. He always let them sleep a lot. They did no work when they got to be that old, and then they just died. Lola was not even sexy, which is supposed to mean attractive. When she laughed, throwing off her gloves, I saw with shock that half of her teeth were gone. Just gaping holes. She looked ill, poor thing, her flesh hung, her ass drooped, and her breasts were large, overused. The kind of breasts peasant women have after they have nursed many kids. I felt bad for her. She looked like she had nobody at all.

Mike ordered another drink and said, "Another minute or so." There were more women on the stage, some blond, others red-haired with different breasts and hips, but all of them did the same wiggling with bras and panties in the orange light while the men around us moaned in pain, "Baby baby, oh baby," they said. Some rubbed their stomachs in the strangest way and looked around as if this were forbidden.

Finally we left and drove once again by the lake, toward the mills and East Chicago. It must have been late, nothing moved on our street. In front of our apartment, in the car, he kissed me hard before he let me go. The hairs on his chin tickled, I laughed. Then he touched my breast which I imagined hard under his hand, like touching a green pear. Imagining what he felt made it almost enjoyable as I added the smell of pears still on the tree in back of my old house. This is more real than my own breasts or being sweet sixteen in East Chicago that summer in the fifties. I didn't know I had become fictional to myself, that I viewed me and him in the car as a scene from different angles, points of view, and I saw what he saw, plus both of us (a two shot) from the back seat — a movie of sorts which had nothing to do with the real me.

Chapter Three

Going up the stairs that night, I wondered if this had been my first kiss or had it been the one under water. Neither, I decided, they were not real. But girls in white dresses on the lake were, and they moved to the sound of rumbas, they swirled with amazing grace, carrying me off to sleep.

What had almost killed me in May now became a permanent dream of girls in white dresses on the lake. I knew I could never be inside that dream, yet a part of me believed that yes, at some future time, I'd get a second chance to catch up and live what had been skipped. Without knowing it, I was becoming American too. Where else in the world do you have anyone believing in second chances and new beginnings?

Mother said casually in the morning that Mike's mother had written — I didn't know they knew each other — and she had hinted at marriage and so forth. To whom? I said, but then she looked at me and I knew. Had she been married this way at sixteen to that horrible man she doesn't want to talk about? Was it all arranged like this? Marriage? Me? Never. I had to be fifteen first, then sixteen again, marriage, what a word, and here I am, a girl who has not even been kissed yet. "What do you think?" I said. "Just watch your step," she said, then and later, her only instructions about men. It was a confusing warning. It meant know them but not too well. That's how I translated it: watch your step. And I was doing just that.

Two men courted me that summer, except that the savior didn't know he was doing it, poor romantic guy. He offered dresses against boys, he only asked for pictures. Mike would want more, no doubt about it, but every time he asked me out I made sure Stojan came along. The savior was not jealous of him; he must have known Mike was not important to me. He didn't count him as a boyfriend, and his gifts of dresses continued.

I soon gave up entirely on the boy at home. He grew dimmer and dimmer, although he wrote a letter every week without fail, with photos of himself against the river and the willow trees. Even the trees seemed unreal, half-dreamt, something out of books, and his words of love and passion produced none of the excitement that I remembered having had once. I stopped writing back, I had nothing to say. Had he kept it ordinary, let's say chronicles of town events, other people's lives, maybe I wouldn't have stopped, but who can tell for sure? The less I wrote the more agitated he grew, until he came up with a frightening proposal — he would find a way to come to Chicago and marry me. Marriage again, me? Even that word seemed foreign, marriage was like death or worse, marriage was what others do. He had it all wrong. He was out of his mind. This seventeen-year-old boy whom I had never kissed was telling me now about the ecstasy of our future married lives and with children! That did it for sure. I didn't even want to think about him. Just thinking about him and children made me ill. I missed only the memory of the fever he had produced in me.

The romance about marriage that seized America around that time, love and marriage and Sinatra singing, and girls dreaming about it — all that was foreign in feeling to me.

Our family life was what it was, days of calm — then an eruption. Our family rhythm. In the absence of friends and relatives, daily gossip and drama that had once enveloped us, had changed — here every small argument exploded because the home and the family were just the four of us. Maybe they argued for entertainment, come to think of it, out of pure boredom, why the old man barked, then beat his dog.

You could never be sure how it began, who said what to whom, or the origin of the fight, you couldn't tell the hidden resentments until everything blew up. Mother never restrained her anger or any other feeling, you got it all full blast, both good and bad, depending on the day. She never forgave him or anyone, that's for sure, wounded in a bad way every single time but never understanding his wounds or mine. Of course, she was not unique in this. Later I would meet people with many degrees who could analyze literature beautifully, patiently examine Madame Bovary or characters in Proust, yet fail to see you in front of them, unaware that their words could hurt. She was not the only one in the family who held grudges, she only brought them up more often and in more dramatic style. The picture of that damn German woman must have come up again, maybe she used it each time she got angry at him; that photo was clear evidence of his wrongdoing, of his betrayal. Our entire nation suffers from that word, past wounds come up all the time, civil war is maybe a family drama, while in the U.S. you just shoot your wife and try to leave the neighbors alone. So, this one time, she must have said something awful to him, she was capable of it, but even she was surprised at the outcome. She said, "He's gone crazy. Do something."

Dad looked strange with his blanket, his head covered with a wool scarf, and he slept this way outside our apartment, in front of the door. It was sad and funny at the same time. I thought then and now of certain Russian novels without being able to pinpoint which character he was. One of those humiliated, forever wounded guys in Dostoyevsky? She worried, predictably, what would people say, what if the old man opened the door, what if the couple downstairs saw. "He'll be the death of me," she said. She always had all those petty bourgeois worries; they were why she never beat us in front of the neighbors, not like other people whose kids would yell and scream and you saw

146

the father's belt hit. No, we were hit only inside the house and told to be quiet about it or we'd get it twice. This way her image remained untarnished in front of the others, and later she even altered, rewrote the bad parts. Worried about the scandal, she said, "Go talk to him because he won't talk to me."

Wrapped in his blanket, outside the door, Dad said he didn't want to move from his spot, he said he would stay there and die like an old dog. "That's what I am," he said, "a tired old dog." He looked like a child, a small orphan boy all curled up, and I thought he had always been an orphan, always would be. I didn't know what to do, what to say. "Nobody cares for me," he said. "Nobody. I wish I could die." I began crying. It was unbearable. I wished I could die too. Instead I said, "It's not true. I do. Please get up."

"She told me she never loved me, not even when we met," he said. His tears and his red cheeks made me think of Stojan when he used to cry. She probably told him the truth, she had always said she had never loved a single man in her life except her father and he of course was strong, dark, and tough.

"She just said that. It's not true," I lied.

"She told me," he began; then he put his arms around me and sobbed. My father was crying in this sad way, a blanket around his shoulders, she was who she was and I was supposed to understand them, love them both, be a grownup. It wasn't fair, I was just a kid, and nobody knew all the sadnesses I had accumulated in me. Plus, I didn't even have a name for all of them. That was another problem.

The old man howled suddenly and threw something across the room, it went thud like a shoe. The commotion helped;, Dad got up and went inside. Mother was very quiet, both of them were. Afterwards we had peace until some new drama began, so much for Hollywood endings, the illusion of a breakthrough.

Chapter Four

Even his secret was small, the kind that never left real echoes, unfinished, amazing dramas you didn't know but wanted to imagine. But he had one of a predictable sort; nobody should have been surprised. It was there before we came, that's why he said all those things about dancing to me, teaching me how to do the foxtrot in the kitchen. "They don't know anything, don't look at that," he would rage against teenagers on the bandstand matinee shows, "let me show you how it's really done." Since we didn't have a record player, he hummed the tunes, all sorts, and, predictably, Mother sneered, "Look at an old horse trying to dance, he who didn't let me do it." She claimed he never let her, too jealous to see her in another man's arms. She said she really missed it, not having had an opportunity to learn. However, since I had never heard this before and she had been free to learn without him all those years, I don't think it was a real desire, more like a wish.

I don't know how she found out, did they start calling or sending the bills but that was impossible since she didn't speak English, and we had no phone. The first time must have happened after church when some guy said to Dad, "How come you don't go there any more?" Dad frowned and tried to change the subject, but it was too late. Mother got curious, and the guy must have spilled the beans. Arthur Murray's studios, that's where he snuck in once a week, telling her he is working extra hours, that's why he knew all those steps, an outrage for a grown man. She was shocked by the amount of money it cost, she couldn't imagine spending it for tangos. Of course he had to quit, except quitting Arthur Murray's was not simple. According to them, he had made a written promise, he had signed up for so many months, and he had to pay up. They were going to sue him, and letters started coming, menace in each. Poor Dad hadn't known about all this when he went there, he hadn't read that sentence in the tiniest letters at the bottom of the page. With the help of some guy, they reduced the sum, but he still had to pay quite a lot and for nothing. He didn't go any more, he couldn't; his magic of dance had died. He would have been humiliated and dishonored had he gone back there after all this trouble, and then he hadn't expected them to behave the way they did. That's what hurt him the most. Arthur Murray's ballroom with nice music, correct steps, was a special place, clean, finely lit, a refuge from East Chicago and America in general and he was wounded that he had liked it so much. "They were so nice to me," he kept saying, "and so elegant." After that he really had nowhere to hide.

His secret didn't interest me at the time, it was all of a piece, and it was over. He didn't talk about it again, and neither did we, my brother and I, while we continued to wonder and question my mother's life, and I interviewed various relatives over and over again, searching for the missing parts. Only when I became a writer did his secret find me, and I imagined him going to his dance lessons from his factory job. It must have been hard; he had to shower and then change into different clothes. Where did he do it? Did he keep the clothes at Arthur Murray's, or at that crazy man's place? He had to take a bus to get there and a bus back. He was tired. How did he manage after eight hours in the factory? I wonder who he danced with, were they good, was he, did he have a drink with them afterwards, was he very different from the person we saw? He had to be. With all her imaginary stories, with a past that escaped us, my mother didn't have another life, you couldn't imagine her as a different woman, a complete stranger.

Chapter Five

If the pain of my first year is still a guide to the memory of real life, the second one is much harder: the pain refuses to come up. The smell remains, the odor of girls' washrooms, pancake make-up and powder, certain lipsticks from five-and-ten-cent stores, or cheap perfumes they don't make any more. I chased after that woman on the subway in New York because her perfume was from that era but I lost her to the uptown train, and just as well, imagine if I had said, lady, don't be afraid, I just want to smell you, that's all. People are scared these days, of anything and anyone, and the trains are full of the sick and homeless thinking out loud. I should have saved something, a perfume bottle, a lipstick, at the bottom of a trunk. I still recollect that very strong, very unpleasant odor of a permanent called Toni, the only one I ever used and only once, given to Barbara and me by her mother, who wanted to improve us. That smelly white liquid transformed my head into tight curls and gave me a look everybody else had. It was called poodle hairstyle. I can't remember now where my hair was cut except that Dad was opposed to it and lost. It was not something I wanted to do, but I was not against it, I must have said why not to Barbara's mother, that's all. I also began wearing red, very red lipstick and my face without it seemed dreadful; I too went into the bathroom with other girls after lunch to add another layer of red, to blot with a tissue. Funny how you get used to things and can't remember what your old face was like. However, I didn't put on gobs of that chalk make-up or powder like the others, and besides I had no pimples to cover up. Mother said pimples came from the goo, and maybe they did, since I'd never seen pimples like theirs at home where everybody's skin was same as mine. Dad said the air caused it too, he said the air was full of poison here. He was not happy that my large forehead was reduced and now covered up with bangs making me look less distinguished. Big foreheads were not considered cute at that time. Now I too wore a bra. I had to. They stared at me too much. The girdle I refused, it seemed like a prison for your hips, and girls were always pulling it down, tugging at it, even in the halls. Why are their asses so big, I always wondered, obsessed with their fat, like a puzzle to solve, and since it was so simple

I didn't see the cause — cars, and more cars, and cupcakes, chocolate bars. In the nineteenth century, in the old photos, Americans looked like us. Their expressions were different too, serious, eyes a bit astonished, no smiles or teeth.

I looked at myself in the mirror constantly, anywhere I saw one, and it wasn't in adoration but to know if I was I. (I have noticed the same symptoms in me recently, when Yugoslavia fell apart, and I would be surprised when people recognized me on the street. After months of the civil war, to me I was another, much older person.) I also looked at clothes constantly, bathing suits, blouses, dresses — in the stores I tried them on, expecting some kind of relief, so when I think about that time I often think blue dress, a blouse with ruffles. I, who used to read at least one book every week, have not read anything for over a year. Did my brain shrink? I began shaving legs my too, just like other girls in the magazines. Armpits too. It was bloody. It hurt. I've quit since. When I look at my old pictures now they don't look like me, and I don't remember what thoughts I had as the camera clicked. The savior's camera, of course. Hundreds of pictures of me, in black and white at first.

Men's eyes produced no effect on me, no shyness or anything you might call "a crush" that girls talked about. Their eyes were wrong, yet I didn't know or forgot what kind of eyes I used to like. At the same time, I half-liked their eyes, or the desire in them, absent in mine. Freedom is that, I believed — not to need anything at all. But unknown to me, slowly, I became this make-believe girl, what the others saw. Without clear likes or dislikes to define me, nonexistent, I could move in and out, sample, get along, later in college go out with football players one night, bohemians the next, and so on, and none of it mattered very much. I was in a movie of my life, and they were the supporting cast. I got engaged in the same way, why not?

The letters from old girlfriends continued, on thin airmail paper so they could write more, it would cost less, in ink, on both sides, with stamps of men and women building roads and bridges their sleeves rolled up. I didn't write many. I sent my dresses instead, bathing suits, nylon blouses. I had more than they. Some friends told about their loves, and vacations on the seashore, Dubrovnik, Brae, some worked the whole summer with volunteers from the entire country to help build a road that would go from Zagreb to Belgrade. This one was to be the biggest achievement, a highway called a beautiful name, 'Brotherhood and Unity', Slava wrote. It sounded wonderful, one more thing I had missed. Next year they'll be on a new road, the first one to connect all the towns on the seashore, and after that the new town in the north. Everyone was helping rebuild what the Germans had destroyed, they were going to make our country a garden of happy healthy people together in socialism. That's what my teacher said in the first grade, she said our tomorrows would sing. They went on year after year, building bridges, railroads, towns — all young, optimistic, eager. Later they would be known as 'the heroic generation' while in '91 another generation went on to destroy everything — bridges, towns, and themselves. My friends said they were sleeping in tents. The food was so-so, but the best part was the various boys they had met. Slava was in love twice that summer — once with a boy from Macedonia, once with a slightly older one from Bosnia. Could he ever sing, she said, what a voice! And how he danced, he made your head spin.

David wrote too, all laments, how could you be so cold, so indifferent, what happened to you? he cried, but his sadness remained on the outside of me and so did the stories of my friends' loves. The pain never entered; there was no jealousy or regret; these letters was as fictional as my life. I was adjusting. That's what adjustment was. We were adjusting, all of us.

We were adjusting so well nobody noticed we had stopped dreaming. This was an important activity at home, retelling our dreams over coffee every day, searching for the meaning of a dream in the morning. Mother dreamt of snakes often, obviously a hidden enemy, but who? I dreamt of swimming and horses, and Stojan had many dreams about apples and other fruit. The dreams foretold the future, what to do, what not, some people in the dream as in life were bad luck, you tried to avoid them, nobody wanted to dream about meeting a priest on the street. And there were good dreams — to dream about a king or a queen, about swimming in clear waters, of finding your house full of shit — this last meant sudden prosperity, while clear water indicated your health was good. This was so important that neighbors discussed their dreams over coffee, uncertain about the meaning, and would change their plans if they dreamt about a priest or a nun. Sometimes girls saw in a dream the man they would marry, and my grandma knew because of a dream the exact day she would die. All this we stopped. And we didn't even notice we had stopped. It took years before my dreams returned, but by then I was no longer in Chicago.

We stopped cooking in the old style, soups, vegetables with a bit of meat. Before, one small chicken was made into four or five dishes to last a whole week. Not any more. Just one night. We couldn't find tripe, kidneys, brains, not even soup bones, we didn't make our own yogurt. We now ate a lot of meat of the sort you didn't have to simmer for a long time. Just slabs. Boring. I missed not having enough; when everything tasted better. And it was more interesting. Sudden surprises when so-and-so killed a lamb for a wedding and sent a piece of meat for us, or when a dam was let out and you caught fish with your hands. We stopped making jams from different fruits you had to gather, like rose hips, blackberries in the fall, we didn't dry various herbs that Grandma used to cure sleep problems, stomach aches, coughs. All the winter preparations stopped — wood-buying and wood-chopping, putting tomatoes, putting up fruits in the jars — this was no longer necessary. And of course we didn't buy a piglet, then fatten him up to give us meat and lard for the whole year. It was food and all that went with it that stopped. And different foods in each season, the anticipation of spring and summer, the first taste of fresh peas. The taste of an ice cream cone in the summer, a rare, special occasion, it wasn't cheap. We had a gallon of it now in the fridge and could have it any time, as much as we wished.

We didn't notice this, it was gradual. We couldn't notice; we lived. Same with the clothes you bought and discarded; in East Chicago, clothes were cheap. Imagine throwing away a perfectly good coat which could have been turned or remade into a jacket, and my old dress would always become a blouse or a skirt. Even when everything was worn out, all the good parts were cut into thin pieces, sewn together and wound into a spool, then a woman across the river would make rugs for us, our old clothes under our feet. You could look at the rug and remember all sorts of things, what you did or thought wearing that skirt. We had winter rugs of wool and spring ones of cotton, and both were washed in the river, dried on the stones. We didn't notice either that our days, the way we lived, had changed. A brand-new dress didn't produce any special joy now, although I expected it to. I didn't stop to think that at home it had been made slowly by my dressmaker, fitted over and over again with gossip, with stories, and then it was the only dress for that year. All that was part of the joy of the new dress.

155

I almost forgot — deciding which fabric to choose for color, the feel of it, the texture, deciding on the cut with the dressmaker, Mother's friend, who laughed a lot and whose son was very handsome. I didn't think about all this. I was adjusting.

We stopped doing many things, all sorts of rituals, celebrations of big and small events, weddings, funerals, the first day of the spring. Big fires in the woods, jumping across them. We didn't whitewash our apartment as we had done every year in May, an important activity women talked about. I think we forgot or half forgot how to behave in the old way, how to dream with no reserve, fully. We were afraid to dream and afraid to fall sick. We didn't go to a dentist as before, or a doctor; our eyes were not examined every year at school.

None of this happened overnight. It was slow, sneaky, it worked on you, it ate chunks of your old soul leaving you bare empty, eroded, so you could adjust better. To what?

Stojan began lifting weights when he saw a photo of a man who looked puny one day and powerful the next. It was Charles Atlas advertising. Unused to all this, he took it seriously, just like when the Albanians in 1990 saw their first American dog-food commercial — everyone in America lives well, they decided, if dogs ride in brand new cars. They rushed to leave their country on crowded ships but landed in Italian camps. The Russians have been complaining lately that they've been had, they didn't think they would get what they got. So it's no wonder Stojan took Charles Atlas seriously; he must have wanted to be powerful real bad. Every night he sweated, ate all sorts of vitamins he had to purchase by mail, each pill as large as half of my finger. For months he went on like that, huffing and puffing, solitary, not talking, painful to watch, and for a while nothing changed about his body because he ate twice as much, but as the iron pieces accumulated in the kitchen, one day, thanks to the savior's picture, we saw that his biceps had grown larger, his thighs too. A bit, that is. Not like that picture in the magazine. With some exercise it would have happened anyway. He had grown much taller, his pudginess had gone. At this point he didn't need anything extra from Atlas, and there was no room for any more metal on the kitchen floor; Mother said enough is enough. However, the Atlas people didn't see it our way. They wrote to inform him that he had signed something or other and it made no difference if he quit or not. He had to pay the total amount or go to jail. We had to pay it all, a large sum at that time and only four months after Dad's dancing lessons! Mother kept saying she'd go mad. From all this, we learned that you had to be careful in America, they'd cheat you on every corner, words like 'honor' or 'giving your word' were worthless, didn't exist; the country was too big. This was the reason those men never married, too scared to marry American women who'd divorce you in a few months. They knew someone who had been foolish enough to try. It's a strange country they said, easy on the crooks, you can rob or steal, then you just skip town, change your name and your profession — you become someone else any time you want. Over and over again, they told stories about a Yugoslav criminal who escaped from jail over there to became a well-known millionaire in Nevada. They said money talks, just money. When the cops stopped us, the savior always said, "That guy wants something for his lunch," then gave him ten or twenty, and that settled it. Usually in Gary, Indiana. He said that's how you do it, it was cheaper than a ticket in the long run.

I can't remember my classes that year, not well, there is a thick fog about everything. My memory is not attached to sounds or smells you could revive, individual days are gone or have merged, my feelings were blunted. I don't remember the exact day I was forced to drop advanced algebra because Mr. Murphy didn't like having girls in his class. He told me so himself the first day. He said it all the time. I used to be good at math at home and I had already had this before, it was not hard; but his daily teasing, the only girl in class, was affecting my other grades so my chemistry teacher advised me to drop it. He saw me crying in the hall afterwards, after all the teasing and all the misery Murphy had caused me, picking on me first, laughing about my sweater and my skirt, and all the boys laughing like fools with him.

157

It must have bothered me, it had to, and a bad grade to go along with
it, that's what happened if you dropped a class after a month. There
had to be other girls before me who could not take Murphy's class, and
yet nobody had ever talked to him about this problem, why didn't they
try to fire the creep? It didn't occur to me to try and argue my case with
the principal. Murphy would deny everything, he would ask the boys
in his class to back him up, and they would. That's how it was. I never
understood why he did all this, because he did not dislike me outside
of class, he would smile at me in the halls. After I left. Why then?
Because I was a girl? Or because I already knew the math problems
in his class and was foolish enough to think he would be interested in
my questions about infinity? Mathematically, I had tried to solve the
puzzle of America and my loneliness in equations I made and showed
to him, as my teacher, to add to, to reject, or to improve. He said
nothing. Were they any good? I had always loved math but that was
my last class ever, I got scared from then on. He died of cancer, that
one, I heard he suffered a lot. I always wished he would. Funny how
that wish was granted, and to this day I don't regret wishing it.

Typing was another misery, and there was nobody to blame. It was
harder for me than for other girls in class who simply went at it without
blinking, their fingers perfectly poised. That's what they would do after
graduation for a year or so before the first baby arrived. They said so,
they said typing would help with the mortgage and things for a year or
so. I can't say it was rebellion on my part, I tried and tried and wished
I could do it. Dad bought me my own typewriter so I could practice
at home for hours, the same boring letters over and over again. It was
hopeless. All my efforts looked like a scene from Chaplin, because the
moment our teacher said 'start,' at the beginning of the one-minute
test every day, all my keys got stuck, my machine even broke down
twice. They gave me a brand-new machine, but it didn't work well for
me. The teacher couldn't believe it, he had never seen that many keys
stuck or destroyed. I think I was terrified of his special alarm clock, a
large one he carried in his hand, I was obsessed by the seconds moving

very fast, fast. Without those deadly seconds rushing to their end and that deadly cry 'start' and another equally horrible 'stop', I would have learned to type instead of getting my worst grade, can you imagine me with a C? That's what I thought at the time but am no longer sure. Maybe it was just too boring for me, the way bookkeeping was the following summer when the owner of a shoe store promoted me from saleslady to bookkeeper, a better paying and somehow more dignified job he thought for a girl who was going to college. I created pure hell within days, my bookkeeping was so amazingly bad he couldn't believe it, he had never seen anything like it, and yet I liked algebra and math, problems to solve. Bookkeeping was boring, the way typing was, the way money is boring for me, just making it. The way college was boring, and so are most jobs.

Other classes were uneventful — English, glee club, library, never ending assemblies every fucking week when we were herded into a large hall and the entire school swore allegiance to the US. A thunder of voices, a hand on your chest, a principal and Miss Winters in front, both looking like ghosts. Then the anthem sung by the glee club. I stand up with others, a hand over my heart, but I don't swear anything with either my mouth or my heart, and nobody knows. They didn't swear anything either, most likely their minds were on boyfriends or cars, anything, that's why those things were such a waste of time. I never liked that melody either, impossible to sing, too high, and those words "say can you see," made no sense at all. "America the beautiful" was a prettier tune, but how could you sing about beautiful landscapes in East Chicago? And I've never liked national anthems in general, it is blood and more blood and victories and if you think that every country is urging people on with horses, heroes and swords it's no wonder we have constant wars.

That year, my senior year, was dominated by its coming end. Around me, giggles intensified, whispers, tears — almost a hysteria about two major events — the winter formal and the spring prom. This was their last stardom and drama. Nobody spoke about college, but about jobs at the mill, "good money," where their parents worked already. Most girls wanted to get married fast, boys wanted a big new car. That was the dream — four, five kids, a house, and the car. Their dreams didn't extend beyond East Chicago, nobody spoke about Europe, even New York seemed very far away. They wanted everything steady, a steady job, a steady boyfriend as soon as possible, how could they want so little, I wondered on and on. Their dreams didn't include others or changing the world. It was just one family inside a house or a car, and ideally the houses and cars would be big rather than small.

I lost Barbara that year as she stayed behind in my old sophomore class. She had her own crowd now; she must have imagined I had mine. Around me more and more girls went steady, with rings and jackets; Slava had a boyfriend too, she wrote, but she didn't understand anything I told her about the necklaces American girls wore with rings dangling in front. She didn't understand either how could I skip two grades and go to university so soon. I'd always be like that — ahead and far behind in everything ordinary — having a boyfriend, a friend, a country, someone. Ordinary would become foreign to me for the rest of my life. Later, I craved it the way some wish for unusual events, extreme states. Those I understood in life and literature as a matter of course without the need for drugs. A capacity to watch, observe others, developed at that time, a form of total distraction even when what I watched was not in itself interesting. The world around me was not fascinating, but I made it so, it was better than nothing, I could get absorbed in it the way I used to lose myself at home in the leaves or grass. And again, from this position, I watched her too, the girl with red lipstick, as she crossed the street, the way she sat down, how she looked at the gas stove sometimes. It was both real and not real — a real make believe, or like real life fiction. It was better than nothing, that's for sure.

A surprise at my first football game, a real shock. Everyone screamed, standing up. In front of us, in the muddy field, boys in scary costumes and helmets crashed into each other. I screamed too, thinking they'd break their bones. To my surprise, they continued for another hour this way and nobody died. Just one game, and no more, never again, just that one. I sampled things. For some, once was enough. Others I repeated to make sure.

"Give me an R, give me an O," the cheerleaders cried, dressed in white and purple skirts. That was the main ambition for girls at Roosevelt High, to become a cheerleader at fifteen or sixteen, and if they didn't make it they cried openly in class. It was also good to wear the boy's team jacket with a large letter R. Which meant they were more or less engaged, and since those boys were the most popular in school, girls wearing their jackets were too. The very best was to be going with a football hero, to be a cheerleader, and at the same time a queen. A queen of something or other, a winter formal, a prom, a queen of this or that game, etc. Queens each had a crown and two attendants, one on each side; they sat on floats that were made and decorated over many months. All three girls wore white strapless gowns called formals, except that the queen also had a crown and a fake silver scepter in her hands. All the queens were either cheerleaders or girlfriends, I observed. There was no doubt in my mind that I was prettier than any of those dumpy queens. It was obvious; a mirror told me. In fact there was no comparison between me and some ordinary, dog-faced girl or the one with lips that were hardly lips or the one with a nose like a ski jump, the favorite American nose in the fifties, the favorite at school. It wasn't a real contest of beauty or grace but something else — popularity or some other idea that they imagined to be pretty at Roosevelt High. They couldn't even recognize a really beautiful girl or they would have picked Melinda, a Mexican girl with amazing coal black eyes and the longest, the shiniest hair, or Genny, my friend, who looked and walked like a real queen. These other queens were a part of everything else, football games, assemblies, a way to pass the time. It didn't bother me that they didn't pick me, in fact something would have been wrong if they had. But this other omission was weird, and forget about unjust and just — I was the only one who had skipped two grades and yet nobody nominated me for the honor society, and can you guess why not? You were supposed to — in addition to having good grades — belong to all sorts of clubs, the more the better. This was called character-building, what character, I wonder? Did it bother me at the time? Not much, once I decided all this shouldn't be taken seriously. Besides, I had been the best in all the classes at home where you had some competition, and we had studied Latin and Greek. It didn't bother me that I wasn't asked to be a silly queen either, because I knew I was one. The savior said so.

Everyone was surprised on Valentine's Day (its meaning unknown to me), right after lunch hour, minutes before classes started, when everyone could see, the savior showed up in front of the school to deliver the biggest heart anyone had ever seen, a heart as big as half of me. Inside were chocolates of all sorts, a silk brush, a comb, and a music box that played a waltz. I gave the chocolates away; I still have the music box and the brush.

My chemistry teacher said, "You'd better join some clubs if you want to get in college. Why, what do clubs have to do with school?" I argued, but he only said, "Don't ask, just do it." So, like it or not, I had to join. He said I had to look normal for that application and list something called activities. Without activities I would be a loner, not a good thing to be. Like Dad? He said why not a book club, and I said fine. It didn't mean you had to read or do anything. I had belonged to the Pioneers, the only club at home for kids, except that was much more serious — you had to be a good student and behave accordingly, plant flowers, assist others, never be selfish or greedy and help build something called Socialism. The book club didn't demand as much. The purpose of it was to improve the Roosevelt High School library through 'service rendering', said Miss Reed, the librarian who was unusually ugly, but kind. The poor woman took care of the library where nobody ever came of their own free will, they were assigned to sit there every day for an hour (and they called this a course), or some were sent to it from some other class as punishment. My guess is that the school hoped to teach the kids how to use other libraries later on, not that they succeeded then or now because the very spirit of books, is foreign in a country with a strong push toward the concrete. This is me now intruding on my young life when I didn't think this way, half-mute, I only listened and looked.

The library was a sad place where the boys who were forced to be there looked like caged beasts; they stared ahead not blinking, waiting for the ordeal to pass. They didn't even see poor Miss Reed, who had a very strange face which might have been less strange on a guy — large chin with a dimple thrust forward, butterfly glasses, a lot of bones. Her skin must have been very pale, and she covered it with pink make-up of the stage sort through which you saw her large pores. Her thin hair, the color of a ripe carrot, was of a slightly different shade from her make-up, and she wore small scarves around the neck—yellow, lavender, red — a different one every day. These scarves you could get at the ten-cent-store for fifteen cents; they were very popular at school as a form of decoration worn with sweaters. Girls also wore long glass necklaces, which dangled between their pointy breasts, and they played with them when talking. Sometimes they tied them in one large knot. See, I remember after all!

In my book club we didn't discuss or read a single book. It was actually a make-believe club to justify the other, more important one — a pretend president, officers, treasury, and so on. There were about fifteen of us, all girls, we stayed for an hour while Miss Reed talked about the importance of books, the secretary took notes and read the notes from the previous meeting. Nobody once mentioned a book they had liked, I was disappointed too when I couldn't find a single Russian writer as I had hoped to do, thinking that maybe I could try to read them in English, since I knew the story part already. Later, I saw that a club like this was to train you for other clubs in the future, taking notes, minutes, etc, a form of social life or a perfect waste of time, like committees at Brooklyn College where I taught for eight years. A way to kill time and to give the impression you were doing something. Nobody became friends as a result of that club nor at Brooklyn College, where committees grew, multiplied, more and more every year, were considered more important than teaching, and my own suggestion to form a committee to work on ending the others was seen as an antisocial act, which maybe it was, or perhaps it was just that my requirements were bigger. I didn't like conformity of the American kind because I didn't know or feel the reasons for it, the aim.

At home we had it too, but I didn't reject it, since it had to do mostly with living together, communal help in good times and bad, and yet an individual was freer than were Americans in the fifties. Much much more, free to dress without girdles and bras, free to have all sorts of thoughts, to walk barefoot in the summer and all that, in a country called a dictatorship. We didn't have dictatorship about the body, the misery of the forbidden, it was viewed casually, without shame, like the seasons, like all living things, like air. It was a pleasanter culture to grow up in — come to think of it, maybe that's why we didn't have all those pimples, or maybe the air was purer.

One club was not enough for my college application, so Y-teen Club was another one I joined. Looking at the yearbook and our pictures now, I read that the club was defined like this: thirty girls elected from the general membership. It's a lie. I had nothing to do with any general membership, nobody nominated me or elected me; my guess was that for some reason they had to have this number, thirty, and they just didn't have enough, so they asked me, or my chemistry teacher forced them. Why thirty, why all girls, why no black girls? The same girls appear in almost all the clubs, all seniors. If you think that a book club was a waste of time, in this one we did nothing at all except pose for a picture for the yearbook. That's it, I swear. For the photo we were to float candles across some lagoon to show that it was our senior year. Something having to do with dreams and so forth. Even though it says in the book it was a lagoon, let me tell you, those dumb candles floated in a large dirty puddle in back of the school, the sort of puddle they call a sink hole now. In the same yearbook in front of me, still kept as a reminder, it says that to belong to the Honor Society you had to be in the upper third of your graduating class (which I was and more) but you also had to have other qualifications — service, leadership, and character. Those three words that would appear later in various other places, in colleges, and jobs, have always mystified me. Service at Roosevelt and later meant you kept busy busy with things, but went no further, leadership at that school nobody had or dared express, the same word in my grown-up life meant giving suggestions or undertaking initiatives of the approved sort. So, in fact, school teaches, taught hypocrisy from the start, the illusion of change and participation. Character — having one was a big mystery nobody could explain. I asked. I think they were as puzzled as I was. What does it mean to have 'a lot of character?' Could you not have enough? Could you have too much? And the strange illusion that you could 'build' it. With what? Imagine a character-building course. English is weird, Dad was right.

The honor society at R.H. had three main activities my senior year — one, decide on a float for the homecoming queen; two, plan something called College Night; and three, the annual lunch at the Rotary Club. Writing this, I am aware of two different voices, that girl was not angry the way I am now. My anger grew with the new words.

There were other similar clubs, each with a president, a secretary, and a treasurer, but I joined only those two. They were all the same, only their names were different. The Teen Council planned the dances after the football games. Girls' Counselors made dolls for orphans and arranged a fashion show and a senior farewell breakfast. These were white girls' clubs; boys went for sports. What the black girls did I don't know. Looking through the yearbook now, I see black students in large numbers, especially in the lower grades.

Winter formal. Winter formal was all that the girls talked about, and if nobody asked you, you didn't go. They worried about it as the dance approached, they cried as I wondered why, why is this dance so important, so what if they don't get invited. It's just one night and no more. What I didn't know, how could I at that time, lost as I was in the middle of all this, that all these things — football games, dances, cheerleaders, queen of the prom — were the final stage of their youth before the boys started working in the mills and the girls put on maternity dresses. That's how it would be. I didn't understand their torment. How could I because my own youth hadn't even started or had stopped at fifteen. However, because this kid asked me to go to the winter formal, I did what had to be done, I said yes, and we, my entire family went from store to store to pick a strapless white gown with layers of lace petticoats, white satin shoes to match, and it all seemed too expensive and it was — to wear for just one night. No one in my family said anything against the purchase; they considered it necessary more than I did.

I didn't know this boy who had a head like a bullet and almost no hair except for a cowlick. We had never talked before although he was a senior too. I don't know why he had asked me. The night of the formal, he came to our house with an orchid, a flower all the boys had to buy, and he placed it on my wrist. It came in transparent plastic box with a special elastic band, which was very constraining. The savior was there for the occasion; he didn't want to miss it although he looked sadder than usual as everybody admired my all-white costume. He took pictures which I still have, of me alone and with Stojan and with Mother. I said to him privately, "This doesn't count; he is not my boyfriend; it's only something you have to do." Then I got into a large blue car with another couple in the front seat. This was called a double date. I had never spoken to them before. All in all, it was weird. The things I had to do in order to adjust.

The dance was in the gym, which had been decorated by one of those clubs, so it didn't look like the gym any more. It was called 'Fantasy in Frost' and everything was pure white, sparkling with imaginary snow. They had done a good job, it was very beautiful, a set for a ballet. Girls fluttered about in gowns similar to mine, in white or pale blue shades, and boys in rented suits, hair slicked to one side, walking funny because their shoes were brand-new. There is not much I remember about this event after this. The boy I was with couldn't dance; when he tried, he stepped on my feet and soon there was boredom and discomfort, I felt crippled in my shoes, which were two inches high. Why is anyone nostalgic about this time? In the car, after the dance, still with that other couple in front, going somewhere, the boy with the cowlick stuck his tongue suddenly into my mouth and I almost gagged. It was surprisingly unpleasant — his mouth had a very unpleasant odor of bad teeth and the worst was I couldn't say much or get out of the car. In college, I learned this type of kiss was called French kiss and apparently you were not supposed to do it on the first date but on the third or fourth. Maybe he invited me for this reason, all those stories about my dancing must have made his head spin. My dancing was called 'hot' a strange adjective for a dance or a girl. Nobody said a hot boy, he is hot. English was peculiar.

I never went out with him again and we never spoke again. Maybe he had to get his own ritual over and done with, to kiss someone the way he thought he had to, maybe it was easier to do it with me. A French kiss rather than an American one. However, the same person told amazing stories later on, how I kiss like a wild woman, French kissed that is, and on the first date. It didn't bother me; I knew what I knew. I was sad, however, that at sixteen and a half I still had not kissed anyone. Those other kisses did not count. A kiss under water with that chubby boy, with an older man, and now this one, the worst of all, which made me feel yucky, and I rinsed my mouth over and over again that night.

The winter formal dress for which we had paid all that money was folded and sent home to make someone happy. And it did, apparently. Funny how little it took. How lucky objects are, all the dead things, you dust them or wash them and they are brand new, clean. If I remembered nothing it would be the same for me, move on and on, eternal present and eternal future, is that what they mean when they say 'the American dream?'

Chapter Six

Who could say why this other boy appeared, even though we were never introduced. It probably had to do with that article in the papers, the one that told the lies about my struggle against Communism and that I am an accomplished dancer. Or the stories about me at school or his own desires. I was not an accomplished dancer but since they said so and since I was better than others, I became one. That is, I did not fight them or explain, I let them believe what they wanted to. It was easier that way. "That's how you do it in America," a filmmaker once said to me at Yaddo, "First I hung up the shingle; then I learned the trade." I had been questioning him and others about the American soul and that amazing idea which is a form of ideology that you can become "someone else." It was for a book I was going to write. He said, "Sure you can, all the time." It didn't occur to me that I was doing it too, a little bit, because at home only trained ballerinas are called dancers and the word writer has a different meaning. I am a writer too, people say in New York, and then you discover they have written diaries or they have many ideas for a screenplay. At least I always knew that my training was limited even though I studied dance for years later on, I knew I could not be a ballerina, nor did I ever say I was a dancer by profession. I said I danced, that's all.

Anyway, this boy didn't want to kiss me or go out with me or anything usual. He had bigger plans for us, we should combine our talents he said and break into show business. He knew what that was.

He was short, powerfully built, with slanting green eyes and very high cheekbones and his eyes remained wistful even when he laughed. Just like those men on the steppes in Soviet films. He said he was Jewish, which didn't mean much to me, good or bad. Maybe he was the only Jewish boy in school; nobody except him had ever mentioned it, but you just don't know. Maybe he was lost too in the midst of all those Christians, I at least had no religion of any sort, nothing I was aware of. Mother's view of Jews was simple: they cook with goose fat; we do it with lard; both of us suffered in the war; and they make very good husbands. Why? She didn't explain. Sam knew exactly what was to be done, he said. He would lift me with one hand with his powerful muscles, I would wear a bathing suit, and we would do all this on Lake Michigan, in winter, on ice and, he claimed, it was just a matter of time until we were discovered. He wanted his muscles to show, he assumed I wanted my legs known, and that's all there was to it. I appreciated his honest approach, it seemed fair to combine our forces and I saw no reason to ask him about details. I didn't quite know what he meant by "discover," a word I knew in connection with Columbus discovering America or Madame Curie discovering something in the lab. But why would anyone want to discover us — did we have something special? He had probably read something or seen a photo in some weight-lifters' magazine and then he had added his own dream to the picture. It's all a question of time, he said and then — Hollywood.

They liked him at home because he was not different from us. He loved everything Mother cooked and he cleaned his plate, didn't refuse if she gave him more. His mother baked some of the same pastries, babkas or strudels, he had good manners Mother said but I knew that she would still say no to Lake Michigan on ice. Heaven forbid, she will

catch pneumonia, she would have said, and then chased him out of the
kitchen. We told nobody for that reason. We practiced our act in the
parking lots, fully dressed, and he would lift me with one hand while
I struck poses with one leg bent, the other one extended, pretending I
was a bird ready to fly. I'd seen some of the poses in a film about circus.
We did our rehearsals about three times, and then we went for the real
thing.

Fortunately there was nobody at home when he picked me up in
his old car which rattled and had flames painted in front and around
the trunk. I had my lavender bathing suit on, but he said no, we had to
do it right. He had ordered from some magazine bathing suits for both
of us, black, silky, and French style. His emphasized his butt, mine left
my stomach bare; there wasn't much to it, top or bottom.

We drove and drove, past Gary and the steel mills, jazz on the
radio, past the beaches I had seen before, and then the lake opened
up more, a vast, white, frozen sea. Wealthy people lived here, he said,
pointing to invisible houses hidden by the fir trees, and when we are
in Hollywood we'll live in places like that. Further out still, the houses
disappeared completely and the cars. In The Dunes National Park,
the sand was covered up with snow, everything empty, and it merged
with the lake, white and empty too. Nobody anywhere, just us. An
occasional shrub held to the ground and was bending under the wind.
We were completely alone. I didn't know what the next step would be,
since it was his idea to break into this show biz, he must have had it
all arranged. I had decided that show biz had to do with singing and
dancing on television and half-expected Ed Sullivan to greet us. I never
understood his expression 'to break into show business' and always
imagined it like this: we are sitting in front of a TV at home when the
screen breaks at home and we fly through the broken window onto
Ed Sullivan's show and land in front of him. I always imagined him
delighted, scared, and surprised, and then somebody had to sweep all
that glass.

Sam turned the heat up in the car, then he oiled himself and me, so we wouldn't feel cold, he explained. He also had two nice identical bathrobes in the prettiest shade of gold. Wearing these and oiled, we stepped into the snow in our bare feet, then ran toward the ice on the lake where we were to perform. The wind took my breath away as he lifted me up just as we had rehearsed it, then spun me around in one mighty hand. His muscles well-oiled looked bigger, more beautiful, than when he was dressed. He had a perfect body, small hips, smooth olive skin. I don't know what I looked liked, only he would have been able to tell. But, something had gone wrong. There were no photographers anywhere in sight, weren't they supposed to be there to take pictures of us? Too bad nobody saw us, how beautiful we were. Nobody, nobody was there not even the birds. It was that cold. I can't say I was disappointed. Ed Sullivan was less real than this. The whiteness of ice, the luminous blue sky produced a sensation of magic. Held by his hand, spinning, flying, I was closer to the sky, didn't feel cold at all. We must have looked marvelous on that lake, too bad the savior wasn't there to snap at least one picture of us, both in black suits, both of us blond, oiled and swirling. How come nobody came? He probably didn't even think about that part, he must have assumed they would by magic suddenly appear. What do you expect? His parents were immigrants too, and he was not American yet. Eventually, we began to feel cold and hungry, and our show was over. In a drive-in restaurant we ate non-stop, then he said hopefully that next time we had to be better prepared, that's all. This was just our first performance, he said, there'd be more to come. Maybe he just wanted to hold me in his hand, maybe there wasn't more to it, I think now.

He came again to tempt me with another brilliant idea — a car race in which I was to sit next to him. He said he had really souped it up, and we would win. Win at what? I wondered, not understanding how this would lead us to show biz. Of course I said nothing to Mother, she would have died from worry, and I went because it was better than not going. That was becoming my motto, a guide.

Sam had gone to a lot of trouble to find and borrow two leather jackets, and we wore black slacks the way you are supposed, to according to him. We looked movie-picture perfect for this role while the others, all boys, were dressed in their usual clothes, dirty blue jeans. Some chewed gum, others toothpicks; all looked a bit edgy. The race was in back of a drive-in restaurant, on a dirt road near Whiting. I didn't know this was forbidden to do. First, I was surprised that there were only five or six cars, and then I saw there were no photographers looking for us. Our car broke down moments after the start, a lot of smoke came out of it, then the flames which we didn't see right away since they were smaller than the painted ones. We had to leave the dead car in back of the drive-in, another racer took us home. He dropped me a block away from the house; nobody noticed I was away. I was learning to lie.

I lost sight of Sam, he either graduated or dropped out that winter, or maybe he went to Hollywood; maybe he is there right now. I hope so. Maybe he'll call me too. His picture is not in the yearbook with the graduating class. Nobody knew what happened to him and his family; he had no friends at school. He was there for a short time, they said. When I called, their phone had been disconnected. Since his family moved a lot, I later imagined all sorts of things; but you can never be sure.

Sam was replaced by others. In addition to the popular students, there were a few invisible ones, all those who didn't belong anywhere, didn't go steady, didn't fit, had no clubs; and I was somehow attracting this bunch. Like David with glasses who wore gray slacks, well-pressed, a sweet boy who never said anything to me until one day in the hall. He whispered, looking around, that he too liked ballet, very, very much. That's how I learned this was a forbidden desire for boys at Roosevelt High.

"Would you like to come with me?" he said the next time. He had it all arranged, which ballet and the night. He specified that he didn't have a car. For some reason this was called 'a date,' while what I had done with Sam was not. I decided that 'date' had to be something very special, that you have to go somewhere —just talking wouldn't be a date. We walked to the elevated train platform a mile away, both of us dressed in 'semi-formal' clothes, both blue from cold. At least his legs were warmer, I had to wear nylons and low-heeled black shoes which offered no protection against the snow, but matched my black skirt and my black sweater, which had one large rhinestone in the middle. I imagined this a suitable costume for a ballet. In Chicago. We had to walk some more, wind whistling all around us. Swan Lake was all white and cold too, a magic of time suspended. We had coffee afterwards; we acted dignified as if we did this every week; back in East Chicago, he thanked me for the lovely evening, he said I was the only one who could appreciate *Swan Lake*. It was lovely, the dance and the set and the opera house, yet I was not the right girl for this ballet, I would have preferred a warmer dance, sunnier, with bare feet, maybe with drums. Why drums I didn't know. I thought of drums as warm.

Was he gay? Who knows. Nobody at Roosevelt High spoke about such things and the word gay eluded me until the sixties when a young dancer told me he was gay and I said, 'How lucky you are. I feel rather sad myself."

An inner moment: sometime in the spring of that second year, walking on Chicago Boulevard away from school I understood everything they said to each other and about me. It felt as if I had absorbed the language overnight. I remember the moment — the world appeared bigger, fuller and yet more cluttered. It was preferable this way, but I could hear myself better before it. You get used to the world of sounds without the interference of meaning. Their words were intruding on my thoughts. And if you don't understand you can always imagine, and most of the time the content is more interesting than what they were saying to each other and about me. There is nothing more to be said about this very important moment in my life while trivial events could be told in great detail and with a story.

I can't remember the day or the year when Stojan and I began speaking English with each other nor do I remember how we sounded before. It had to be different. Some words are not translatable, some don't exist, like special endearments, like many different kinds of rain, or that expression my aunt used when she would say, "Ah, my soul is black! Oh, my soul is heavy."

Then out of a clear blue sky, Bonavatura arrived on the scene, or rather he was always there except I hadn't noticed him. With only months left before we graduated, he said he didn't want to waste his time on Elks dances or the American Legion, he had more interesting things on his mind — to know me, if only for a brief moment in time. I regret I didn't see you dance, he said, but let's not cry over spilled milk, and besides my spies have told me enough. I can tell a talent when I see one, he said, introducing himself one day in the hall, grinning widely, looking like nobody else ever. Everything about him was unusual, his clothes, his face, and his speech. He wore extravagant suits, some almost white, always with a bow tie, very clean dress shoes, and his hair was combed back in waves, shiny from brilliantine. I don't know how he managed all this at Roosevelt High, most likely he had a special role of a court jester and comedian. He never slouched or looked bored, many years separated him from the rest of us; he looked like a thirty-year-old talent scout, or a film producer, he smoked cigars — Bonavatura was a disk jockey, and he did magic shows for orphans in his spare time. This was a man Sam should have known, not me.

His face was as unusual as the rest of him, perfect creamy skin untouched by the sun, well-shaped delicate mouth, arching eyebrows, very beautiful nails. You could not imagine him in East Chicago, you expected him to burst into an old aria from Rigoletto or something of that sort, and he did just that one day, with all the gestures of the small-town Italian barber in a movie I saw. His family was from Naples; they loved music and pretty things, and for that reason he hoped I wouldn't turn down his offer, to be his assistant. He had done magic acts since the age of twelve, at weddings, hospitals. My part was easy — grin and be yourself. He showed me how to smile — that is, smile for no reason at all, just to show your teeth. He explained that in show biz and the

U.S. there is no other way; it means you are friendly and you like everyone, plus I had pretty teeth. I practiced grinning, afraid Mother would see me and think I'd caught Dad's disease. I practiced walking in high heels.

It was best not to tell them at home about any of this, and so I invented a story about going to the library with Barbara while Mr. B. waited for me two corners away, in a raincoat and sunglasses, carrying an umbrella he needed for his job. I helped him with magic by walking across the stage in my bathing suit, waving all sorts of scarves, distracting the audience this way while beautiful white doves flew out of his sleeves. Sometimes he sawed me in half while the kids screamed or he found eggs in my hair and none ever broke because they were not real. He was a happy man, not a boy, and loved magic and everything magical. He said he wanted me to dance for the school's biggest show, at the end of our senior year when you could do anything you wanted for 'Show Down,' once in your life. My job was to dance and invent the story too; he knew I could do it or he wouldn't be wasting his time. As a producer, he would be at my disposal with everything, if I said yes he would find me any music I wished. He was the best producer I would ever have; he didn't question or try to alter my vision. Like a perfect parent, he was there to help everything along. I began thinking about the show. For starters, I told him to find me something with drums.

We were interrupted by College Night, an event which was not well attended. It was less important than a winter formal or a prom, in an undecorated, gray-looking gym. Nobody had told us what to expect, what to ask. There were many forms — you fill out this and that, and then there was money. The reality of money dominated College Night. It was a shock to discover how much it would cost to go to the University of Chicago where, for some reason, I wanted to go. I had seen it once with Mihailo, Mike, and the seriousness of it appealed to me, old gray buildings, in Gothic style, grungy students, men with beards, girls with no make-up. I would have had a very different life there, probably would have met people like myself, might have 'belonged,' but who could afford it? Not us. The tuition was more than what my father made in a year. I couldn't qualify for a grant; you had to be an American citizen first. Maybe there were other grants we didn't know about, just as we didn't know about other schools and wouldn't until later on. At that time, I didn't know about Harvard or Columbia or any other school in the East, nobody ever mentioned them at Roosevelt High, but they would have been expensive too, no doubt about it. Maybe that's why they didn't talk about them to us. It was accepted, they knew you didn't go to Harvard from East Chicago. It was so foreign, so impossible that nobody even wished for it or was disappointed. I didn't want my parents to feel bad; so I never mentioned the University of Chicago. Still, the Roosevelt High paper wrote another proud piece, after College Night, OUR GIRL MAKES GOOD, it said and the girl was me. A college in Iowa offered me a full scholarship, everything paid, for some mysterious reason. Why?

The school in Iowa was serious about everything (why? I wondered, why me? what did they see in me? did I say something special?), they sent a husband-and-wife team to take me there for a visit, in the middle of a snowstorm, beautiful snow I remember in Iowa, big drifts, intact, clean. The school was very orderly, sunny and clean too, everything peaceful, students polite, girls without make-up. There was one catch, I realized: in addition to my other subjects, I had to take Bible class every semester, and then there was daily chapel. My reaction to the Bible was rather extreme, the way Devil responds to the sign of the cross in books, but there was more to it, I think. The chapel in the center of the campus dominated every aspect of its life, and my fears, the sudden lack of air, were simple pagan fears. I don't remember what sort of chapel it was.

I said no to them in a letter, politely, and began filling out forms for the large state university, the cheapest so far, except for the extensions. Going to college was considered special at Roosevelt High, unusual, out of reach, and they kept saying how lucky I was to come to

America where I was free to do all this. They were probably repeating their parents' words but I was irked. I failed to appreciate my good fortune because I would have gone to college at home, and since I was a good student, the state would have paid for it. I did not understand why I was so lucky, so free. Actually, since I wanted to go to a school that had been eliminated for no other reason than money, I felt less free than if I had gone to a university at home, where only those who passed the entrance exam could go. I mention this because I grew up under a different system; Americans did not ask questions like these. They didn't ask for longer vacations nor could they afford a doctor except when very sick. I never understood why. They didn't even see that some were more free than others at Roosevelt High. Freedom to choose is wonderful if everyone can choose; otherwise it's only a dream, a nice thing to say in the Constitution. My chemistry teacher had wanted me to escape to some better world but I didn't make it, not then. Instead, through no fault of my own, I was heading to a school I knew nothing about, the one I did not choose, where beer and fraternities dominated, girls were 'pinned,' and where you could be called 'different' for no apparent reason. It was enough you didn't go to church on Sundays, if you wore a black sweater instead of a pale blue or green one. There were things you were supposed to say and not say, and if you had friends of a different race, it was not very good. If you violated these unspoken rules, you were punished in many strange ways. I didn't know about the Klan before I.U. I didn't know the real meaning of class either and when I did it struck me as unfair, unfree, and a bit funny, as a caste system of sorts. Can you imagine girls examining your dress for a label and judging you accordingly? And all this in a country that kept talking about freedom at a time when Americans were sadly unfree, though sadly, they thought they were, so it resembled the mind of a very sick person. I always thought of America as a permanent adolescent who had been a very gifted child and then somehow became deranged, failed to mature.

177

Chapter Seven

"She is not going to college," Dad announced one day at lunch, without looking at me. "See, right here, where I have to sign, I'm not going to do it," he said, jabbing the application form with his finger.

It made no sense. If anyone cared about books, he and I did. He wanted me to go, he had always talked about it; it was taken for granted and now this. Most likely it had to do with an argument they had had, and this was his futile attempt at winning. He should have known better. Just a hug would have changed everything, a gesture she reserved for Stojan who still sat in her lap once in a while.

"Just go and try," she said to him," go ahead. I'll sign and pay for it. I have a job." She was working in a restaurant now, later she switched to cleaning floors.

"Nobody cares for me in this house," he said, slamming the door. "I'm just an old donkey, that's all." He forgot his sad lunch, which he always prepared himself, just bread and butter and coffee. It had to be just that, done his way and nothing extra. He claimed that with all the dust in the factory, this was all his stomach could take. And now even that remained on the table and that sinister lunch pail I hated so much. Even now, when I think of that day and that lunch of his, the pain in me is bigger than anything I could name. He didn't have time to look back like the rest of us, to change, rewrite, re-examine. He never knew I cared for him, although I probably didn't know it at that time nor the meaning of that word love.

That day, I probably worried only about me and college. This at least was taken for granted; of course, I would go. Now, in addition to all the other nagging thoughts that I'd missed everything in life, I had to think about this too, and endure total uncertainty about right and wrong, what was the best to do. And her own rage at not living well, worse than she had at home. America hadn't delivered for us, we couldn't hide and pretend, we knew we shouldn't have come. Her own disappointment was so huge, she, who used to be strict about life and morals, now repeated daily a kind of litany, "Go out, have a good time, youth will pass. I was dumb, so dumb, go live, live." What does it mean, "live, live"? She never explained how to do it. I interpreted it to mean only what I was not doing now. These words, "live, live" I came to associate only with extreme states larger than life, like fever, like dance, like drums, the opposite in my mind to marriage, and family because they were linked to her temperament. She didn't intend it that way, she didn't think carefully about intentions or results, her main aim was self-expression, and since she didn't keep track of her thoughts, she could change her mind. Later on, I associated "live, live" with Carmen, one of my favorite characters. There weren't that many women who lived well in fiction I realized, who else is there besides Carmen, and even she gets stabbed.

Instead of living, I made do, always knowing which is which, no confusion ever about that part. And since I had to do something after all, I didn't say no to this sweet shy boy who began walking me home. Instead of being very different from her, as I imagined I was, I was only following her advice. He carried my books, and we must have looked like a picture of two perfectly normal American kids in the fifties —

my hair was blond, my eyes were blue; he looked cute and blond too, and there was nothing wrong with him except that I wasn't interested in him in that special way his eyes wished for. All this must have been communicated to him, and he told me a friend of his really loved to dance and could never find the right partner. It was so generous of him to suggest that we should meet, how unusual, how kind he was at that age to accept everything, to see it all without a grudge, or extra words. In retrospect, he was the most timid of all the seniors, and the wealthiest too — his parents didn't work in the mills, his father owned a movie theater and a gambling casino. Nobody was well to do at Roosevelt High, nobody spoke about money or parents, the way they did later at I.U. So, Harold must have been like a displaced person too; in spite of his father's murky connections, he didn't know how to speak rough, curse, or talk about cars and sports. In his well-pressed gray slacks and pale blue cardigan, he was the opposite of what girls found attractive at that time in East Chicago. In a nicer place he would have done fine, would have been considered good-looking too. Walking me home after school he said, "I'll tell him to call you."

"We have no phone," I said.

He looked at me; it was unheard of.

"My father doesn't believe in phones," I said. His theory was that you don't need them. If people want to see you, they'll just come or they won't, and that separates the true friends from the others. He didn't believe in cars either; it was healthier not to drive. He never drove. I didn't tell all this to H., who, to his credit, received the information about my lack of a telephone in a way that most wouldn't have in East Chicago. He perceived us, me, as original, nothing to be ashamed of. It's no wonder that, of all people, many years later I could talk to him about that time and us, in San Francisco, where he lives now. He is still generous, kind, the way he was then, when he told his friend to come and see me because I would like him better because we could dance, which he couldn't do.

So, this boy called Bruce showed up one day after school together with H., who introduced us. He asked for a date, "It's a date," he said, and I registered that this must be my second date so far although he was the first one to use that word. Going to a ballet was the first. As I said, I imagined 'dates' as having something to do with going out to exceptional places, and sure enough he said we would go to Roseland, a famous dancehall with many bands in Chicago. Dancing is what he wanted to do.

He didn't look like a dancer, for reasons I couldn't explain. He was blond, bland, thin, with the kind of hairstyle known as the brush cut; all his features were clear and sharp. He also had a smell of peppermint about him, a different smell from that of other boys at school, and he made it known that he lived in the suburbs where they had houses with big yards and well-tended grass. But he still couldn't find someone to dance with out there and had to come to East Chicago. I couldn't imagine him dancing. Looking at him, I finally understood the meaning of 'clean cut' and also 'a well-scrubbed look'. My second year in America the ugly brush cut didn't bother me anymore; in general it separated good boys from hoodlums who had haircuts like Elvis. Elvis had just made his appearance on the Ed Sullivan show, and girls screamed like crazy. In my kitchen, we remained indifferent to Elvis and most other stars. Father and I thought he was vulgar; Mother liked only Liberace; Stojan said nothing. James Dean was the first American actor I paid attention to. I had the impression, looking at him and his eyes, that I was seeing his soul and that I was seeing myself. His loneliness on-screen appeared huge.

At home nobody said no to Bruce, mostly because Mother had become my defender now — live, live, live and all that — and by now they were getting used to many strange practices in America. They saw it as a necessary evil, connected to school, and doing well in life, they had to say yes to outside activities or I wouldn't get my diploma, and my mother wisely gave up on her old rules — she had decided that I knew best what to do or what not to do. We had broken the old rules long ago, my girlfriends went out, had boyfriends — always one at a time — but the boy never entered the house or that would be serious. It meant involvement with parents, getting engaged. They would meet on the street, at night, by the river, much better, less embarrassing than the American way of doing things.

A new kind of embarrassment seized me for the first time when Bruce knocked on our door — I saw us with his eyes: black stove, ugly table and ugly red chairs, kitchen full of cooking smells, onions, garlic. All I needed was an extra detail, and it happened — the dog began howling next door. It was horrible, my entire family gathered, all three shook Bruce's hand. Didn't they know you don't do this in the US? Fortunately, I was ready, and off we went to Roseland, to dance in Chicago.

For this occasion I wore a black skirt of a modified flamenco cut, twirling at the bottom but tight around the hips and the waist, black flats, and a white jersey with sequins around the neck. I can't remember his car or him or very much about Roseland except its size. Too many people, hundreds; too many bands, too metallic somehow. Brass. The music didn't tempt me to dance, and besides the two of us couldn't dance at all together, can you imagine! It was strange, he either stepped on my feet or I stepped on his, and we just couldn't get what's wrong with our feet and our arms. The truth was so simple — I could only dance alone, inventing my own steps, or with someone who had the same rhythm; he was strictly Arthur Murray, the precision Dad would have liked. It had to be this way and only this way. I don't think he listened to the music at all. In the absence of dance, we necked and kissed (funny that word "neck"), and kissed some more in the car parked in front of our apartment. The response of my body was huge, a fever, I was alive again after a long time, I wanted it to last, and yet I knew it might not. Please, I prayed to whomever, let it go on. It wasn't him I had in mind, but me. I had not fallen in love — his face was nice but no more.

Love, that word meant different things, love the way Slava wrote about it or the way I imagined it, always there, never an English word, love is only a translation of the other word, which is bigger and thicker and darker in my language, love was about a face, a person who entered your head and couldn't be dislodged. I was not in love. My body liked Bruce, that's all.

He came again, but we didn't go to Roseland. We sat and kissed in his car. Is this what dating was? I had no girlfriends to ask about things, and Mother didn't ask any questions or offer much information on this subject.

Bruce said he would like to take me to the prom, an important event in three months from then. I didn't give it much thought. It was fine, they said at my school, he could take me. I had to get permission since he was from another school. They were surprised, impressed that he would drive all the way to East Chicago, considering that they thought he lived in a nicer town, and went to a nicer school. And that's not all. Bruce wanted some change, poor guy, we didn't do anything except sit in his car. He suggested some more middle-class entertainment, like church. This was his attempt to bridge our differences, tell me about his family, or to move us into the larger world away from his parked car. I am sure his intentions were good.

For this occasion I dressed in what I imagined an American church costume to be —a blue silk suit with long sleeves, a white hat and shoes; I even wore white gloves and must have looked truly delicious. Grace Kelly wore a similar costume in one of her films. At home they knew about this event for a week, it was a part of their entertainment too; they watched and approved the colors of white and blue. Then, ten minutes before he was to arrive, just as I sat down ready to wait for Bruce, Dad said, "She is not going, she can't."

"Why?" I said. "You said I could."

"I've changed my mind."

"He is coming to pick me up," I said. "Any minute now."

"You are not going to their church."

It was crazy. He was not religious. We seldom went to our church.

Then Bruce appeared — blond, polite, with that brushcut or whatever it was called, and he smiled just the way you are supposed to. Dad in his old flannel shirt, unshaven, looked like a madman, like a homeless person, even more when he shouted at him, "gerare, sir," which was supposed to mean 'sir, get out of here!' Bruce understood nothing until Dad opened the front door and pointed his finger in a dramatic way learned from silent films. Bruce said nothing; he looked at us for a long time and then went through the door. I started after him, to tell him, to explain, but Dad seized me by the shoulders and slapped me hard. Then our usual Sunday happiness began.

His ways were peculiar. The following week, he said calmly, in a matter-of-fact manner, that I could go to that American church if I really wanted to. Whether he changed his mind because she had persuaded him or because he had won this one, I'll never know. His permission was irrelevant, Bruce didn't invite me to his church again. The event sealed things between us. I didn't see him again, although he insisted he had to take me to the prom as he had promised he would, a gesture that was honorable, joyless, and absurd. I wouldn't have done it in his place, but then I never understood middle-class puritan virtues or lies. For example, he never said, "Look, I can't go out with you anymore because you have no phone and your family is rather nuts." He said instead that he lived too far away, and besides we'd be going to college, and so on. I wasn't hurt at all; I was even getting a bit bored with our necking in the car. I was grateful to him, glad that I had managed to kiss someone after all. I only wished that he, a perfect stranger, hadn't witnessed our misery.

Chapter Eight

Since the short interlude with my "boyfriend" Bruce was over, everything except the prom, I could devote myself to bigger things — show biz with Bonavatura. He was secretly glad that he wasn't seeing Bruce any more — obviously I had sent him packing to his boring world, he chuckled. I said nothing; there was nothing to say. I didn't miss him, not even a little bit.

We began rehearsing in the gym, even though the story wasn't ready yet. The music provided by B. was a marvelous piece he had stolen from some Brazilian composer, drums and drums, moments of peace, then larger and smaller eruptions building up steadily. By rehearsing the dance steps, or rather by trying to find them, I hoped the story would reveal itself. The music suggested something big, call it passion, call it revolution, call it love .Our costumes would be minimal, simple, in earth tones. No shoes. The music called for it. I kept thinking about rites of spring, a celebration of sorts. It was going in this direction, music, bare feet, the story made itself known.

B. loved it. We rehearsed during lunch hour, the only free time in the gym. We hardly ate. B. chewed on his cigar outside the school. In his white suit, he looked perfect for his role of producer. We had picked Washington, who had the most beautiful, the deepest voice, to sing and tell the story, the village elder, the wise man, and the costumes designed by me would be made by his mother for nothing. The fabric didn't cost much because there wasn't much to our costumes — men wore only minimal, sort of jagged, short trunks; and the girls' tunics were sleeveless, with hems of different lengths. It was meant to produce a natural effect, as if the dancers had lived, slept, swum in the same clothes all the time. We looked good — there was no doubt about it.

It was really an offering to the goddess of spring, and I, as a lost girl, managed to find happiness at the end because I had been absorbed into a wonderful new tribe. Of course, there were other stories, all having to do with love and spring, but mine was at the very center even though I didn't play the goddess. That part we gave to Leila with the bronze skin, who could sing, who was very, very tall and more than beautiful. I thought we were fair, we went by talent alone — I mean to each according to his or her ability. Everyone thought I should play the part of the lost girl who disappears happily in the jungle and the leaves cover her up. The show didn't end there. The drums and the dancing continued faster and faster and the goddess was unable to resist, finally she leapt from her special spot to join the rest of us. Up to that moment she only sang; now she had a real dancing part which Leila did marvelously, timid at first. I thought the entire show was rather Greek in idea, a mix of the human and the divine; the cast was happy. In fact, they were given the roles they wanted to play and the roles they deserved. Washington was a lead singer in his church; his voice was so big, he didn't need a mike. We had no major disagreements; or the only two initial problems solved themselves because the two dancers realized by watching the others that they couldn't do the parts they wished for well. We didn't have to fight about this; they didn't want to look like fools after all. It was participatory democracy at work. "We are good, B.," said, "we are fit for bigger things, New York maybe!" He couldn't stop grinning. How happy he looked!

Our only problem was how and where to rehearse, because sports had priority for the gym after school. We were given just the lunch hour, which meant we had to cope with all those kids running around, curious about us. Finally, we posted a guard at the gym door — nobody was let in, because the show was meant to be a major surprise, but we had to let in the principal and Miss Winters, known to everyone as 'the evil witch'. We had less than a month to go before graduation and our show, but after that visit in May everything was over with.

They called me into the principal's office alone, a clever thing to do. She said, "We won't permit this, not in my school!"

"What did we do wrong?" I said, shocked.

"It's indecent," she said, grimacing. I didn't know that word. "What is indecent?" I asked.

"The dance," she said, "all of you like savages."

"Savages?" I asked. Again I didn't understand, even though I knew that word. We were neither brutal nor uncivilized.

"We won't permit it."

"I thought we were permitted anything for the end of the year." Bonavatura said that.

"No, you are not, young lady! Not the jungle. I won't have any jungle in my school. Did you see," she turned to the principal ,"what they were doing with their hips, have you ever.."

"It's only show business," I said," like on the Ed Sullivan show."

"Not like that, not with hips."

"You can't dance with hips?" I said, astounded.

"And shoulders." The way she said shoulders made shoulders ugly.

"What can you dance with?" I said.

"I am losing my patience," she said. "You can't do it, that's all. We have skipped you two grades. Aren't you going to college?"

"I guess so," I said.

"You still have to graduate, don't you?" She stopped here to look at me and him, and then said, "We could hold you back, couldn't we, Mr. Simon?" He nodded yes.

"Because I danced?'

"Up to you," she said. "You are free to choose."

"Choose how, what?"I said.

"You are irritating me, you are playing dumb!" she shouted.

"I don't understand," I said. I really didn't.

"It's simple. Either you dance or you graduate. It's like that — you are free to choose."

"But what about them, what do I tell them? We have rehearsed for a long time."

"Oh no," she said, "you can't do that."

"You tell them," I said.

They left me to whisper in another room. When they came back, he said, looking over my head, their faces dead, "If you want to graduate, you can't tell anyone about this. We are only protecting our school against disorder. You can't tell anyone. Is everything clear now?"

I believed them. They would hold me back. How could I even think of defending myself after two years in a country we used to know for its freedom, Radio Free America and all. The confusion of it all, and that word 'democracy' Mother loved so much. I didn't even know the meaning of blackmail yet in any language but even if I had, it would not have mattered. They could do things. I was an alien from a Communist country; they could say I had invented everything they had said, they could change my grades, why not? I thought of those people on Ellis Island for the first time; maybe they would take me there. My fears had no limits. I was inside a nightmare now, from that position, mute like a trapped animal, I nodded yes, then went through the door.

It occurred to me to ask Dad for help but I dismissed that too; he would get wired up against everything in this world, he would go to school, and there'd be no graduation for me. This I knew — I would die if I didn't leave soon. The chemistry teacher knew everything, I was sure, but he only averted his eyes in the hall and looked around him as if he too were being watched. Only once he said, "Just think, in less than a month you'll go, think that, less than a month."

I decided to tell Bonavatura the truth; then halfway through it, I stopped. He talked too much, everyone would know. Winters witch watched us; principals' eyes were on him too. I grew scared of something big that I couldn't name. They might hold me back for starters, and then in addition you just don't know what else they might do. I had nightmares, waking up shouting in a cold sweat; briefly I reverted to that time when our house had been bombed and dead soldiers were everywhere on the street. Still, the worst was my own shame, of the kind I hadn't known before, a feeling of cowardice, and that word "compromise" which I would know later and would hate more than shame or betrayal. I was betraying myself, I had to betray myself in order to live through that day when, looking at my feet, I told Bonavatura that my father didn't want me to dance any more. I knew he knew I was lying, but to make him believe my story I stopped everything I loved doing, including our magic show with kids on Sundays. My cast was simply crushed — all those rehearsals, and the costumes which we would never wear. The blame fell entirely on me, a spoiled girl, they must have thought, a superficial creature, she gets us to work, then changes her mind, and here I was trapped, full of rage and unable to kill anyone. I wished, I dreamt brilliant dreams of revenge in great detail, and some were so real I cried from bliss — I had the school burned down, big flames enveloped the principal's office, Miss Winters looked like a roast turkey, and even though the dreams never came true, they were real in my head, they consoled me. It's better if you can imagine, even if it's only pictures, it's better than nothing. Imagine if I couldn't have imagined. But I didn't know the full extent of my rage until much later, when the Vietnam War began or even later still when I watched the L.A. riots on TV. Burn it all down, I shouted, burn it all, and I knew why my own anger is so deep, why humiliations don't just disappear, why vengeance, no matter how small, is necessary. I never compromised again, even in situations where I should have. It was a point of honor, something I had decided not to do. From a nice, what you might call a middle-class girl, obedient, proper, good student, I became a rebel in the U.S. It was not natural to me, I was a good pioneer at the core. The seed was planted in me that year. If you look at the pictures in the yearbook, the first year I was still soft, romantic, wistful, and sad, my hair long, a little Jewish princess almost. The senior-year photo is different — short hair, a defiant face looks at you, sexy on the surface with almost hard eyes, go reckon with me, go try, my eyes seem to say. Dancing doll, it said under my picture.

I couldn't start a fire at school, let's be serious. How would I do it? I needed gasoline and a helper — matches were no good, everything was iron, aluminum, glass. The library was the only place that would catch and the only one I didn't want to burn. The principal's office was always locked up. And there you have it. I thought about the details. If Sam had been around, I might have tempted him with it, he was the only one I would have trusted with this. It was fortunate he was gone, he was not good at details.

I can't remember what skits they did the day of the Showdown, what silly songs they sang. I have erased everything except the very end, the last five minutes or so. In addition to the usual skits, we were permitted jokes and gifts for teachers; Bonavatura was the master of ceremonies in his suit and bow tie. For this final act he had a large bag full of presents in front of him and an occasional pigeon flew out of his sleeves. He didn't look unhappy; his face was the same as always, a cheerful mask; Bonavatura was a pro. He didn't seem to bear a grudge the way I did. He knew nothing, that's why. I wanted revenge and was willing to spend many days looking for a perfect present too, which he announced finally, looking surprised." And this one is for Miss Winters, from Nadja," he read. "Jungle sounds. She says it has to be played and we are going to do just that. OK, guys get ready, here we go."

Apparently, Winters had never received a present before. Giggles erupted. They laughed some more as the music came on. "Mambo, mambo," someone sang in Spanish; then came the drums. Excited by the end of the school year, the kids went wild. Winters must have been shouting but she couldn't be heard. It was nice to see her that way, her face chalk-white, waving her arms, stop it, stop!

Bonavatura let it go on for several minutes, and for a few minutes he too moved his hips until Winters climbed up on stage and turned it off. I think he knew then, or I hoped he did, everything I couldn't say. We never talked about it. I was free now, she couldn't stop me, we had received our diplomas in the morning. I wished the cast could know the truth but I was still too frightened to tell them. Maybe they knew, maybe they guessed it.

Washington said afterwards, the first time we spoke in a month, "Our stuff was so much better, wasn't it?"

"Yes it was," I said, to say something.

"We were in a different league, weren't we?"

"We were fine," I said, "no doubt about it."

"You're something else, you know that? That was pretty good," he said, and began laughing. "Mambo, mambo, I thought she'd have a fit." He got me laughing too, I was so relieved; he didn't hate me.

"Stay cool," he said. Maybe he had it all figured out, maybe. Cool how, I kept thinking, not sure what cool was.

I had believed they stopped us because they didn't like the way we moved. Some of our steps, suggested by the music, resembled African dances, like Dunham, which I saw and studied in New York later on. I didn't see that there was more to it — why it had to be stopped — I was the only white dancer and the only white person in that dance we had invented and I fell in love with the prince whose skin was like coffee with cream. Everyone was invited to audition, to try out for the parts, but the white students didn't come, that's all. B. should have anticipated problems, but he was too caught up with bigger things and colorblind too.

Instead of an African prince, I went to the prom with Bruce, wearing a foamy blue dress and shoes. We didn't kiss. We knew tomorrow we'd part. I didn't care. It was a sinister thing to do. I didn't have a good time or a one bad. It was like nothing, sort of. The savior took pictures of that too.

Later, I learned this indifference so well, I perfected the distance so much, that it felt real. I could laugh, have a great time just about anywhere, but it was always as if in a costume, a play in which I starred while others figured as background noise or walking trees far away. And later still, much later, I saw it like this — in East Chicago I lost everything — Mother, Father, Stojan, my river, even my grandma's voice and my own, that's where I died that night and this other girl took her place, prancing, posing with a freedom most people don't have. It's easy. I wasn't there.

However, she didn't die completely, bits and pieces of her remained, it was she who urged me like a vampire, not giving me any rest, live, live she said, you can make it up. That's how the two of us went to college, one wearing black shades after a car wreck, the other forever fifteen, naive, romantic, sweet, with a mad wish to roll back the years. She tried it constantly, like wishing to be delivered, and succeeded once in a while with the help of music and the perfect stranger on the dance floor or the perfect stranger as the sound gave a background to life, filled all the missing parts.

The girls in white dresses stayed in my head as I remained innocent and jaded at the same time, then around '85 I lost them. America made me into an artist, something I wouldn't have been at home, it was my way to survive, and for a writer it can be useful, this detachment from everything. My life would be much, much more 'interesting', thanks to the displacement. It doesn't mean that all this made me happy, not in the way I imagine that word, happy as a union of parts, body and soul, impossible in this country, not just for me but for others, so hard to be happy if you have constant new needs and disposable souls. What made me different from an average neurotic New Yorker, or many complex people I would meet, some of my friends, is this — they didn't know what it felt to be whole once, and I did. I am not sure if this made me stronger or weaker or forever split. I have never met an immigrant who was not split.

This is where this book should end. It's not a story of my life, just those two years, encapsulated by pain, raw, remembered more than others later on. Others were of a different sort, good and less good, but not like these. Fifteen and sixteen in East Chicago. A story about immigration.

About the author

Nadja Tesich was born in Yugoslavia and came to Chicago at age fifteen. She attended Indiana University and the University of Wisconsin and did graduate work at New York University Film School and the Sorbonne in Paris. She has taught Film at Brooklyn College and French Literature at Rutgers University. She is the author of the novel, "Shadow Partisan" which received grants from the National Endowment for the Arts and the New York State Council for the Arts. Her other published works include:" Native Land" and the play "After the Revolution", as well as short stories and poetry. She has worked in films, and is also the author/ director on her own movie, "Film for my Son. "As an actress she starred in "Nadja A Paris" by Eric Rohmer. Nadja Tesich currently lives and works in New York City

LaVergne, TN USA
14 November 2010
204886LV00003B/180/P